Quick and Easy, Proven Recipes

Snacks &
Street Eats

Publisher's Note: Raw or semi-cooked eggs should not be consumed by babies, toddlers, pregnant or breastfeeding women, the elderly or those suffering from a chronic illness.

Publisher & Creative Director: Nick Wells
Senior Project Editor: Catherine Taylor
Art Director: Mike Spender
Layout Design: Jane Ashley
Digital Design & Production: Chris Herbert

Special thanks to Esme Chapman, Emma Chafer and Frances Bodiam.

This is a **FLAME TREE** Book

FLAME TREE PUBLISHING
Crabtree Hall, Crabtree Lane
Fulham, London SW6 6TY
United Kingdom
www.flametreepublishing.com

First published 2013

Printed in Singapore

All images © Flame Tree Publishing Ltd, except the following which are courtesy Shutterstock.com and the following photographers:
8 Kobby Dagan; 9t Gwoeii; 9b Kevin Hellon; 13b,15b zkruger; 15t happystock; 16t JPL Designs; 19t keng88; 19b Gayvoronskaya_Yana; 20t Sunny Forest; 20b neil langan; 21b Africa Studio; 25b Wiratchai wansamngam; 28t HANA; 29t discpicture; 29b jabiru; 37t Portokalis; 38 Julija Sapic; 85 Paul Horwitz.

Quick and Easy, Proven Recipes

Snacks & Street Eats

**FLAME TREE
PUBLISHING**

Contents

&

Essentials

The recipes in this book are a tasty and versatile way to cater for a whole host of occasions – from parties or picnics to a family lunch with a difference. Before you get stuck in to the cooking, take a minute to learn about the origins of street food and brush up on your exotic ingredients and cooking techniques; it's time to make sure you know your bok choi from your Chinese cabbage and your stir-frying from your shallow frying.

Introduction

༆

So what is street food? Well the clue's in the name really – fresh, fast takeaway snacks and meals that are usually sold to hungry customers on the street, providing great tasting food that can be eaten on the spot for the fraction of the price of a sit-down restaurant meal.

That said, the appeal and lure of street food extends beyond the food itself and the way it is cooked; it is also about the attitude and the atmosphere. Street food markets in busy cities of developed countries attract punters who flock towards exotic smells and vibrant coloured fare to discover a heady assault on the senses which evokes the notion of being in a far flung corner of the world where street food is not merely a way of eating but, for many, a way of life.

Not A Flash in the Pan

According to the UN Food and Agriculture Organization, street food is now eaten by an estimated 2.5 billion people across the world every day. But this eating culture that fills the bellies of such a huge proportion of the world's population didn't spring fully formed from nowhere. Instead, street eats have early roots the world over. From fried fish in ancient Greece, through spit-roasted meat in Renaissance Turkey, to the street food explosion that accompanied urban population growth in Thailand, it is truly a long-established global phenomenon.

In countries such as India, China and Mexico, street food traditionally is the most affordable way to eat, but luckily it is also one of the most tasty! Fresh ingredients and local knowledge passed from generation to generation mean that street food really packs a punch to rival the flavours of even the most pricey restaurants. Nowadays, most people would be able to think of a 'street' food for at least a handful of countries – kebabs in Turkey, burritos in Mexico, noodles in Japan and falafel in Israel spring to mind – but street eats are also incredibly regional, with hardened travellers growing sensitive to changes in local specialities between regions.

A World on Your Doorstep

It is this wealth of national and regional flavours that has inspired the stalls and markets that have sprung up all over America and Western Europe: the street food revolution has hit with gusto, and the trend is set to sky rocket. Reasonably priced and catering to all tastes and appetites, this culture is a thriving effect of a global outlook and multi-cultural society – no longer are authentically flavoured Thai noodles reserved for the wealthy jet setter – instead they can be enjoyed in the comfort of your home city... or even your own home.

Easy to prepare and even easier to eat, the array of recipes in this book give you the means to prepare your very own fresh and flavoursome 'street' eats for the table. With a particular focus on the rich range of South East Asian street foods, this book transports you from your kitchen counter to the backstreets of Bangkok and the sun-drenched shores of Shanghai. With a minimum of crockery required for the cooking, and clean fingers often sufficing for the eating, its time to reach for your spice jar and cook up a street food feast!

　　　　　　　　Introduction

Fresh Ingredients

In all street-food cooking, the basic philosophy of balance is the same, where the freshest produce is combined with the flavours of dried, salted and fermented ingredients, preserves and condiments. Most ingredients are now available in ordinary supermarkets and a few of the more unusual ones in Asian or Chinese groceries and markets.

∾ Aubergines – Chinese aubergines are thinner with a more delicate flavour than the Mediterranean variety. They are used in many savoury dishes and in Thailand, some varieties are eaten raw with a dip or sauce.

∾ Mushrooms – Oyster mushrooms with their subtle flavour and delicate, almost slippery texture often feature in Chinese cooking. Now cultivated, they are widely available. The colour of the fan-shaped cap gives the mushroom its name, although they can also be pink or yellow as well as grey. Tear into long triangular segments, following the lines of the gills, and cook the smaller ones whole. Shiitake mushrooms were originally Oriental, but they are now grown all over the world. They are more often used dried in Chinese cooking, but may also be used fresh – the caps have a strong flavour and are generally sliced and the stalks discarded. Cook the mushrooms gently for a short time, as they may toughen if overcooked. Straw mushrooms are sometimes known as double mushrooms because that is exactly what they look like; two mushrooms that grow end to end. They are small and pale brown with a pale-coloured stem.

∾ Baby Sweetcorn – These tiny, tender cobs of sweetcorn, about 7.5 cm/3 inches long, are crunchy and sweet. When buying, make sure that they are bright yellow with no brown patches, firm and crisp.

∾ Bamboo Shoots – Bamboo shoots are young, creamy-coloured, conical-shaped shoots of edible bamboo plants. They add a crunchy texture and clean, mild flavour and are sometimes available in Chinese groceries, as well as vacuum-packed or canned in most supermarkets. If you buy the latter, transfer them to a container of water once they have been opened. If you change the water daily, they will keep for up to five days in the refrigerator.

∾ Beansprouts – These are the shoots of the mung bean and are readily available prepacked in the vegetable section of most supermarkets. They add a wonderfully crisp texture when added to stir-fries and take only a minute or two to cook. Ideally, the brown root should be removed from each sprout and discarded, however, this is time consuming, but improves the appearance of the dish.

∾ Mangetout – These tender green pea pods with flat, barely formed peas have a deliciously crisp texture. To prepare them for cooking, simply top and tail, pulling away any string from the edges.

∾ Yard-long Beans – Although unrelated to French beans, they are similar in appearance, but about four times longer. As they grow, they start

Fresh Ingredients

to curl and are often sold in looped bunches. Two varieties exist: a pale green type and a much darker, thinner variety. They are very popular and may be found in great quantities in Chinese markets. The Cantonese often cook them with black beans or fermented bean curd and in Sichuan, they are deep-fried. Store in a plastic bag in the refrigerator for up to four days. To prepare, cut into lengths and use in exactly the same way as French beans.

∽ Bok Choi – Also known as pak choi, the most common variety has long, slightly ridged white stems like celery and large, oval thick dark green leaves. It has a mild, fresh, slightly peppery taste and needs very little cooking. Choose smaller ones if possible, as they are more tender. Store in the bottom of the refrigerator.

∽ Chinese Mustard Cabbage – Also known as gaai choi, these mustard plants are similar in appearance to cabbages. The whole leaf is eaten, usually shredded into soups and stir-fries to which they add a fresh astringent flavour.

∽ Chinese Leaves – Also known as Chinese cabbage, Chinese leaves look like a large, tightly packed lettuce with crinkly, pale green leaves. It adds a crunchy texture to stir-fries.

∽ Chinese Kale – This green vegetable is popular in Thai cuisine. It has an almost earthy and slightly bitter taste and is usually served blanched and accompanied by oyster sauce. When buying, look for firm stems and fresh, dark green leaves. Store in the bottom drawer of the refrigerator for up to four days.

∞ Water Spinach – This is widely grown throughout Asia and is unrelated to ordinary spinach. The leaves are elongated and tender and the stems fine and delicate. Water spinach requires minimal cooking. It is cooked in the same way as spinach, either steamed, stir-fried or added to soups.

∞ Chinese Celery – Unlike the Western variety, Chinese celery stalks are thin, hollow and very crisp and range from pure white to dark green. Used as both a herb and a vegetable, Chinese celery is often stir-fried or used in soups and braised dishes.

∞ Basil – Holy basil with small, dark leaves and purple stalks is frequently used in Thai cooking, although sweet basil, more easily obtainable here, may be used instead.

∞ Coriander – Fresh coriander is the most popular fresh herb used in Thai cooking. It has an appearance similar to flat-leaf parsley, but has a pungent, slightly citrus flavour. Leaves, stems and roots are all used, so buy in big fresh bunches if possible.

∞ Curry Leaves – The shiny leaves of the curry tree (*Murraya koenigii*) are important in Indian and South East Asian cuisine, used much like bay leaves are in the West. They can be crushed using a pestle and mortar or fried in hot oil to release their nutty fragrance, or can be torn into shreds or placed in whole at the start of cooking.

Fresh Ingredients

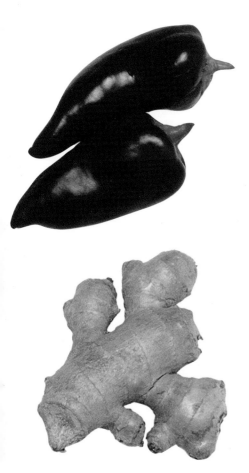

∾ Chillies – There are many different kinds of chillies and generally, the smaller they are the more fierce the heat. Red chillies are generally milder than green ones because they sweeten as they become riper. The tiny, slender tapering red or green bird's eye (or Thai) chillies are very hot and pungent. Cooks often include the seeds in cooking, but to moderate the heat, scrape out and discard the seeds.

∾ Tamarind – This adds an essential sour taste to many dishes. It is extracted from the pods as a sticky brown pulp, which is soaked to make tamarind water.

∾ Garlic – This popular seasoning flavours much of Asian cooking. In Thailand, garlic heads are smaller and thinner skinned, so they are often used whole as well as finely chopped or crushed. Choose firm garlic, preferably with a pinkish tinge and store in a cool, dry place, but not in the refrigerator.

∾ Shallots – Small, mild-flavoured members of the onion family, shallots have coppery-coloured skins. Use them in the same way as onions, or thinly slice and deep-fry to use as a garnish.

∾ Spring Onions – Long, slender spring onions are the immature bulbs of yellow onions. They are frequently used in stir fries, as they cook within minutes.

∾ Ginger – Fresh root ginger has a pungent, spicy, fresh taste. It is usually peeled, then finely chopped or grated – vary the amount of ginger used to suit your own taste.

For just a hint, slice thickly and add to the dish when cooking, then remove just before serving. Fresh ginger is infinitely preferable to the powdered variety, which loses its flavour rapidly. Fresh ginger should feel firm when you buy it. If you have more than you need it can be used within a week. Store it in the freezer as it can be grated from frozen.

≈ Galangal – This is a rhizome, called laos or ka in Thailand. It is similar to ginger, but the skin is a pinkish colour and the flavour more complex and mellow. Peel it thinly and slice or grate the flesh. When sliced, it can be kept in an airtight container in the refrigerator for up to two weeks. If unavailable, ginger is an acceptable substitute.

≈ Krachai – Also known as lesser ginger, this is smaller and more spicy than either ginger or galangal. It can be bought fresh in Oriental food shops or dried in small packets.

≈ Chinese Keys – Despite its name, this root vegetable is often used in Thai cuisine and rarely in Chinese. It is a member of the ginger family, with an aromatic sweet flavour that goes well in Thai curries.

≈ Lotus Root – This is the underwater rhizome of the lotus flower and has a lacy appearance when sliced and a sweet, crunchy flavour. Fresh lotus root takes about two hours to cook, so it is worth considering using canned lotus root instead. It is used in soups and deep-fried, stir-fried, and braised dishes.

Fresh Ingredients

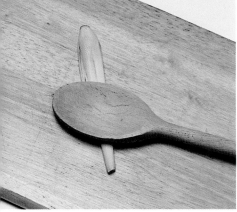

Mooli – Also known as daikon or white radish, these look like smooth, white parsnips (they come from the same family as the radish). They have a peppery, fresh taste and are often used in salads, peeled and thinly sliced or grated. They can also be cooked, but because they have a high water content, they should be salted to extract some of the liquid, then rinsed well and steamed or boiled. They are often carved into beautiful and intricate shapes as a table decoration or garnish.

Water Chestnuts – These are bulbs of an Asian water plant that look like and are a similar size to chestnuts. When peeled, the inner flesh is very crisp. Some Oriental grocers sell them fresh, although canned, either whole or sliced, are almost as good.

Kaffir Lime Leaves – Dark green, smooth, glossy leaves, these come from the kaffir lime tree and are highly sought after for Thai cooking. They add a distinctive citrus flavour to curries, soups and sauces. Buy them from larger supermarkets and Oriental grocery shops and keep them in a sealed polythene bag in the freezer. Lime zest can be used as an alternative.

Lemon Grass – These look a bit like spring onions, but are much tougher. The stems should be bashed to release the lemony flavour during cooking, then removed before serving. Alternatively, peel away the outer layers and chop the heart very finely.

∞ Durian – This large, spiky-skinned tropical fruit has such an unpleasantly strong aroma that it is banned from public transport and hotels in Bangkok. It is expensive to buy a whole fruit, but you can sometimes buy frozen packs of skinless pieces of fruit.

∞ Mango – This sweet, fragrant, juicy fruit is a delicious addition to many asian dishes, sweet or savoury, whether salads, salsas or stir-fries. To test ripeness, press each end of the fruit firmly – if it yields to the pressure then it is ready; if not, it can be left to ripen in a sunny place.

∞ Papaya – Also called pawpaw, the unripe green flesh of this tropical fruit is often used in Thai cooking. It ripens to a deep orange colour and is delicious sliced and served as a dessert.

∞ Tofu – Tofu or bean curd has been used as an ingredient in Thai and Chinese cooking for over 1000 years. Made from yellow soya beans, which are soaked, ground and briefly cooked, tofu is very rich in protein and low in calories. Because of its bland taste it is ideal cooked with stronger flavourings. It is usually available in two types: a soft variety known as silken tofu that can be used for soups and desserts, and a firm, solid white block, which can be cubed or sliced and included in stir-frying and braising. Also available is smoked tofu, which is a seasoned bean curd. When using, cut into the required size with care and do not stir too much when cooking otherwise it will disintegrate and lose its texture; it simply needs to be heated through.

∞   Fresh Ingredients

Store-Cupboard Ingredients

There are many dry, canned and preserved ingredients that are essential to creating the full flavour of asian and worldwide dishes, not to mention the rice and noodles that will soak up all the wonderful juices and sauces.

❧ Beans and Pulses – Many beans and pulses (dried and canned) are used in asian cooking. For example, black beans are small, black soya beans that may also be known as salted black beans, as they have been fermented with salt and spices. Sold loose in Chinese groceries, but also available canned, they have a rich flavour and are often used with ginger and garlic with which they have a particular affinity.

Also, mung beans, lentils and chickpeas are often found in Indian dishes (and the latter in Mediterranean and Middle Eastern food too).

❧ Cashew Nuts – These milky-flavoured nuts with a crunchy texture, are often used whole or chopped in Chinese cooking, particularly as an ingredient in chicken dishes.

❧ Mushrooms – Many sorts of dried mushrooms are used in Asian cooking. Cloud ear (black fungus) mushrooms need soaking in warm water for about 20 minutes before use. They have a subtle, mild flavour and are highly regarded for their colour and gelatinous flavour. Dried shiitake mushrooms have a very strong flavour and are used in small quantities. After soaking, the hard stalks are usually discarded or added to stock.

ຈ Chillies – Dried red chillies are used throughout Thailand and in many regions of China. The drying process concentrates the flavour, making them more fiery. Look for dried chillies with a bright red colour and a pungent aroma. If stored in a sealed container, they will keep almost indefinitely. Chilli oil is made from crushed dried chillies or whole fresh chillies and is used as both a seasoning and a dipping condiment. Chilli powder is made from dried red chillies and is usually mixed with other spices and seasonings, ranging from mild and aromatic to very hot – always check the jar before using. Chilli bean sauce is a thick, dark paste made from soya beans, chillies and other spicy seasonings and is very hot. Seal the jar after use and store in the refrigerator.

ຈ Szechuan Peppercorns – This small reddish spice has a distinct, woody flavour and is more fragrantly spicy than hot. It is one of the spices in Chinese five spice powder. Also known as fargara and Chinese pepper, Szechuan peppercorns are used extensively in Sichuan cooking. Unrelated to peppers, they are the dried berries of a shrub and have a slight numbing effect on the tongue.

❧ Cardamom – A spice with medicinal properties, cardamom is used in Indian curries and rice dishes. Cardamom pods come in green and black varieties.

❧ Star Anise – This is an eight-pointed, star-shaped pod with a strong aniseed flavour. It is added whole to many Chinese dishes, but is usually removed before serving. It is also a vital ingredient in Chinese five spice powder.

❧ Cloves – Cloves have a distinctive sweet, spicy and peppery flavour. They can be used whole or ground and should be used in moderation due to their strength.

❧ Coriander – Ground coriander is made from coriander seeds and has an almost sweet, spicy, fresh flavour. You can buy it ready ground or instead toast whole seeds in the oven and grind them yourself.

❧ Cumin – A regular in Indian curries, this strong spice adds warmth and earthiness to recipes.

❧ Turmeric – This mild flavoured spice adds a bright yellow hue to foods. Although it can sometimes be bought fresh, it is most often used in its dried powdered form.

❧ Garam Masala – A ground spice mixture typically used in Indian cooking, the constituents of garam masala can vary widely but often include black and white peppercorns, cloves, cinnamon, cumin and green and/or black cardamom.

∾ Sugar – Added in small quantities to many savoury dishes, sugar balances the flavour of a dish, and gives a shiny appearance to the sauces. Thai palm sugar comes in large lumps or slabs, which need to be bashed with a mallet, to break into smaller pieces.

∾ Coconut Milk – Rich, creamy coconut milk is extracted from the white flesh of the nut. It can be bought in cans or made by adding boiling water to a sachet of coconut powder. Sometimes an opaque, white cream rises to the top of canned coconut milk and solidifies. You should shake the can before opening. If the milk is stored in an airtight container in the refrigerator it will last for up to three days, however, it does not freeze well. Occasionally, freshly made coconut milk may be bought from Oriental groceries. It is often used in Thai cooking, especially in curries and may also be used in desserts.

∾ Creamed Coconut – Made from coconut oils and other fats, this comes in a hard, white block. It is not a substitute for coconut milk and is usually added at the end of cooking, to thicken a sauce, or to add coconut flavour to a finished dish.

∾ Wonton Wrappers – Also called wonton skins, wonton wrappers are egg and flour pastry-like wrappings that can be stuffed then fried, steamed or added to soups. Fresh ones may be stored for about five days in the refrigerator if kept wrapped in clingfilm.

∾ Noodles – There are many types of noodles used in Thai and Chinese cuisine. The most popular include

Store-Cupboard Ingredients

cellophane noodles – also known as glass noodles – that are white and become transparent when cooked. Made from ground mung beans, they are never served on their own, but are added to soups or are deep-fried and used as a garnish. Egg noodles can be bought fresh, but the dried ones, which come in fine and medium, are just as good. Generally, flat noodles are used in soups and round ones for stir-fries. Rice noodles are fine, opaque noodles made from rice flour and are also called rice sticks. They are common in southern China, as it is the rice growing area of the country. Wheat is the primary grain in northern China and is made into noodles without egg. These noodles are sold in compressed square packages and bundles. Yifu noodles are round, yellow noodles, woven in a round cake and are often sold precooked.

∞ Rice – Long-grain white rice is the most commonly used rice for serving with many of the dishes in this book. Glutinous rice is a short-grain variety often used in desserts. It is sometimes referred to as sticky rice. Thai Jasmine rice is a long-grain rice from Thailand with an aromatic and subtle flavour.

∞ Rice Paper – This is made from a mixture of rice flour, water and salt, which is rolled out by machine until it is paper-thin and dried. It comes in round or triangular pieces which can be softened by placing between two damp tea towels and are then used to make spring rolls.

∞ Rice Vinegars – There are several varieties: white vinegar is clear and mild; red vinegar is slightly sweet and quite salty and is often used as a dipping sauce; black vinegar is very rich, yet mild and sweet vinegar is very thick, dark-coloured and flavoured with star anise.

- **Rice Wine** – Often used in Chinese cooking in both marinades and sauces, rice wine is made from glutinous rice and has a rich, mellow taste. Do not confuse rice wine with sake, which is the Japanese version, as it is very different. Pale dry sherry is a good substitute for rice wine.

- **Sesame Oil** – This is a thick, dark-golden to brown aromatic oil that is made from sesame seeds. It is rarely used in frying, as it has a low smoke-point, but when it is, it should be combined with another oil. It is often added to a finished dish in small quantities.

- **Sesame Paste** – Sesame paste is a rich, very creamy brown paste made from sesame seeds, however, it is not the same as tahini paste from the Middle-East. If unavailable, use smooth peanut butter, which has a similar texture.

- **Sesame Seeds** – These are the dried seeds of the sesame herb. Unhulled, the seeds may be dull white to black in colour, but once the hull is removed, the seeds are a creamy-white colour. Sesame seeds are often used as a garnish or as a light coating to add crunch to food. Toast them first, to intensify their flavour, by shaking over heat in a dry frying pan until the seeds are lightly coloured.

- **Groundnut Oil** – Also known as peanut oil, this has a mild, nutty flavour. Because it can be heated to high temperatures, it is ideal for both stir-frying and deep-frying.

- **Soy Sauce** – Both light and dark soy sauce feature frequently in Chinese and Thai cooking. It is made from a mixture of soya beans, flour and water that are fermented together and allowed to age. The resulting liquid which is then distilled is soy sauce. Light soy sauce has a lighter colour and is more salty than the dark variety. It is often labelled as 'superior soy'. Dark soy sauce is aged for longer and the colour is almost black. Its flavour is stronger and is slightly thicker than light soy sauce. Confusingly, this is labelled in Thai and Chinese food shops as 'Soy Superior sauce'. It is also possible to buy a mushroom soy sauce, which is made by the infusion of dry straw mushrooms and a shrimp-flavoured soy sauce.

∾ Hoisin Sauce – This is a thick, dark brownish-red sauce, which is sweet, tangy and spicy. Made from soya beans, salt, flour, sugar, vinegar, chilli, garlic and sesame oil, it may be used as a dip, in 'red-cooking' and as a baste for roasted meats.

∾ Nam Pla Fish Sauce – This is a golden brown, thin sauce with a salty flavour and is made from salted and fermented fresh fish, usually anchovies. It is used in Thai cooking in much the same way as soy sauce is used in Chinese cooking. The fishy aroma is almost unpleasant when the bottle is opened, but this mellows when mixed with other ingredients, adding a unique Thai flavour.

∾ Oyster Sauce – This is a thick, brown sauce made from oysters cooked in soy sauce. It has a wonderfully rich, but not fishy flavour, as this disappears during processing. Often used as a condiment, it is also one of the most used ingredients in southern Chinese cuisine.

∾ Shrimp Paste – Made from puréed, fermented salted shrimps, this is popular in Thai cooking and adds a distinctive fishy flavour. There is also a Chinese version, which has an even stronger aroma. Use both sparingly. Dried salted shrimps are also available, which are sometimes used as a seasoning in stir-fries. They should be soaked first in warm water, then puréed in a blender or made into a paste with a pestle and mortar.

∾ Yellow Bean Sauce – This thick, aromatic sauce is made with fermented yellow beans, flour and salt and adds a distinctive flavour to sauces.

∽ **Plum Sauce** – As the name suggests, plum sauce is made from plums that are simmered together with vinegar, sugar, ginger, chilli and other spices.

∽ **Thai Curry Paste** – Red curry paste is a strongly flavoured spicy paste made mainly from dried red chillies that are blended with other spices and herbs. There is also green curry paste, which is hotter and made from fresh green chillies.

∽ **Thousand-year-old Eggs** – Fresh duck eggs are often preserved in brine, which seeps into the shell, making the whites salty and the yolks firm and orange-coloured. Thousand-year-old eggs are preserved in a mixture of clay, fine ash and salt. The whites of the eggs turn a translucent black and the yolks a grey-green colour after a year or so, hence their name. Unopened eggs can be kept for many months.

∽ **Cassia** – This is the bark taken from a cassia or laurel tree and is dark brown and flat in shape. It is similar, but slightly less subtle than cinnamon.

∽ **Bird's Nest** – This very expensive delicacy is literally a bird's nest made from the spittle of a swallow. It is harvested from caves or special nesting houses and can occasionally be found in Chinese food shops. It is sold as a crunchy jelly that is often added to sauces, soups and extravagant stuffings and is an acquired taste. Since it is dried, it can be stored in a dry place for several years. To use, it should be soaked overnight in cold water, then simmered for 20 minutes in fresh water.

Store-Cupboard Ingredients

Equipment & Techniques

℮

There are numerous pieces of equipment that are very useful in Asian and street food cooking. Most can be bought very cheaply from Oriental grocers, or often more expensively from department stores.

Woks

The most useful piece of equipment is, of course, the wok. It is much easier to use than a frying pan because of its depth, making it easier to toss the food around quickly without spilling it. A wok also requires a lot less oil for deep-frying than a deep-fat fryer, although more care is required in terms of safety. Another advantage is that the shape of the wok allows heat to spread more evenly, ensuring that the food cooks much more quickly.

There are a number of shapes of wok available. The Cantonese wok has short handles on each side. This type of wok is best for steaming and deep-frying because it is easier to move when full of liquid. The Pau wok has a single handle and is better for stir-frying, allowing you to manoeuvre the pan with one hand while stirring the food with the other one.

Woks can also have rounded or slightly flattened bases. Round-bottomed woks are really only suitable for use on gas hobs. Flattened-bottomed woks can be used on gas and electric hobs but are better for deep-frying than stir-frying.

When choosing a wok, look for a large one simply because it is easier to cook a small amount in a large wok than a large amount in a small one. Choose a wok that is heavy and made of carbon steel, rather than stainless steel or aluminium, which tend to scorch. Non-stick woks are also available but these cannot be seasoned or used over very high temperatures, both of which are essential for flavour in stir-frying. Electric woks are also available, but these cannot be heated sufficiently hot enough and tend to have very shallow sides. They also lack the manoeuvrability of a free-standing wok.

If you buy a carbon-steel wok, it will need to be seasoned before use. First, scrub well using a cream cleanser or another abrasive to remove the machine oil with which it will probably have been coated to prevent rusting. Dry it well and then place it over a low heat. Add a little cooking oil and rub this all over the cooking surface with wadded kitchen paper. Continue heating over a low heat for 10–15 minutes, then wipe well with more kitchen paper – the paper will blacken. Repeat this process of coating, heating and wiping until the kitchen paper comes away clean. With continued use, the wok will darken further.

Do not scrub a seasoned wok with soap and water. Wash in hot, plain water using a brush or non-stick scrubber. Dry thoroughly with absorbent kitchen paper and place over a low heat until completely dry. Rub with a few drops of cooking oil to prevent rusting. If a little rust does appear, scrub off with cream cleanser or another abrasive and repeat the seasoning process.

Equipment & Techniques

Other Equipment & Accessories

∽ **Wok Stand** – If your hob will not support a free-standing wok, Oriental stores sell metal rings or frames, called wok stands, that stabilize round-bottomed woks. These stands are an essential piece of equipment, so if you plan on doing a lot of steaming, deep-frying or braising in your wok it may be worth purchasing one. The stands are available in two designs: one is a solid ring punched with ventilation holes and the other is a circular wire frame. Only use the wire frame stand if you have a gas hob as the other stand will not allow sufficient ventilation.

∽ **Wok Lid** – You may also find it useful to have a lid for your wok. Wok lids are dome-like in shape, are usually made from aluminium and are very inexpensive. Any large, dome-shaped pan lid that fits snugly over the wok will suffice. Alternatively, use kitchen foil.

∽ **Rack/Trivet** – If you are going to use the wok as a steamer, a wooden or metal rack or trivet is also a useful tool, as it holds the plate or steamer above the water.

∽ **Steamer** – For steaming, it may be worth investing in a bamboo steamer. They are both attractive and effective. They come in a variety of sizes and stack together with the uppermost basket having a lid. Fill the steamer with food, placing the food needing the longest cooking time in the bottom basket and the more delicate foods in the top basket. Stand the steamer on a trivet in a steady wok of boiling water. Cover tightly and leave to cook.

- Cleaver – Chinese cooks would not be without a cleaver. It differs from a meat cleaver in that a Chinese cleaver has a finer, much sharper blade and is used for all kinds of cutting, from shredding to chopping up bones. Several types of Chinese cleavers are available including a light-weight, narrow-bladed cleaver for cutting delicate foods such as vegetables, a medium-weight model for general use and a heavy cleaver for heavy-duty chopping.

- Spatula – A long-handled spatula is also an important piece of equipment. Special spatulas with rounded ends are readily available and make stirring and tossing food in the wok much easier. A long-handled spoon can be used instead.

- Rice Cooker – Another very useful piece of equipment if you plan to do a lot of asian cooking is an electric rice cooker. It will cook rice perfectly and keep it warm, sometimes for up to several hours. It also has the advantage of freeing-up cooker space. They are relatively expensive, however, but if you cook rice frequently it may be a very worthwhile investment.

- Chopsticks – Chopsticks are used in Chinese and Japanese cookery not just for eating but for stirring, beating and whipping. They are available in wood and plastic and can be bought in Oriental grocers and department stores. Chinese chopsticks are larger with blunted ends, while Japanese chopsticks tend to be smaller with pointed ends. To use chopsticks, put one chopstick into the crook of your preferred hand, between

Equipment & Techniques

your thumb and first finger, holding the chopstick about two-thirds of the way up from the thinner end. Let it rest on your third finger. Put the second chopstick between your thumb and fore-finger so that its tip is level with the chopstick below. Keep the lower chopstick steady and move the top one to pick up food.

Preparation Techniques

The initial preparation of food in this kind of cooking is probably more important than the cooking itself. Most dishes are cooked very rapidly, so it is important that everything is prepared beforehand and is chopped into small, even-sized pieces to ensure quick, even cooking without overcooking. This type of preparation also ensures the dish looks attractive.

∾ Slicing – Several different types of slicing methods are useful, including the conventional method of laying the food firmly on a chopping board and slicing straight down to cut the food into thin slices. Meat is always sliced across the grain to break up the fibres and to make it more tender when cooked. If you use a cleaver, hold the cleaver with your index finger over the far side of the top of the cleaver and your thumb on the side nearest to you and guide the cutting edge firmly through the food. With your other hand, hold the food and make sure when cutting that you turn your fingers under for safety.

∾ Diagonal slicing – This is particularly useful for wok-cooking vegetables as it exposes more surface area to the heat of the wok and also makes the food look much more interesting. Simply angle the knife or cleaver against the food and slice. For larger vegetables such as courgettes, carrots and aubergines, make one diagonal cut at the end of the vegetable. Turn the vegetable 90 degrees, cut in half lengthways, then diagonally slice each half. Continue until the whole vegetable has been chopped into even-sized pieces.

∾ Horizontal or flat slicing – This is a technique for slicing whole foods thinly, while retaining the overall shape. A cleaver is particularly useful for this technique. Hold the knife or cleaver with the blade parallel to the chopping board. Place your free hand on top of the food to be sliced. Using a gentle slicing motion, slice sideways into the food and right the way through, taking care to keep your upper hand out of the way. This is particularly useful for splitting chicken breasts and similar meats.

∾ Chopping – This is the simplest technique and refers to simply cutting food through. With whole birds or cooked food with bones which needs to be chopped into smaller pieces, place on a firm surface, then using a straight, sharp, downward motion, chop through the bones, hitting down with the blade, then finish off the blow with the flat of your other hand on the top edge of the knife or cleaver. A heavy cleaver or knife is best for these tasks.

∾ Dicing – This is a simple technique of cutting food into small cubes or dice. First cut the food into slices as for

∾ Equipment & Techniques

shredding. Stack the slices and slice again lengthways into sticks, again as you would for shredding. Turn the sticks again and cut crossways into cubes.

◦ Shredding – This is cutting food into fine, matchstick shreds. First cut the food into slices, then stack the slices and cut again, lengthways this time, into fine shreds. It is sometimes easier to cut meat and fish if they have been placed in the freezer for 20–30 minutes before slicing.

◦ Mincing – This is a very fine chopping technique. First slice the food and then chop it rapidly – it will spread out over the chopping area. Gather it into a pile and continue chopping and regathering until the food is chopped as finely as needed. If very fine results are required, a food processor may be a better tool to use, but be careful not to overprocess.

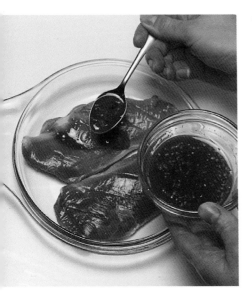

◦ Scoring – This is used to score the surface of foods, such as duck breasts and squid to help them cook faster and evenly and to give them an attractive appearance. Use a cleaver or sharp knife and make shallow cuts into the food at a slight angle. Take care not to cut all the way through. Make cuts right across the food, then turn and make a second series of cuts at an angle to the first set to make diamond shapes.

◦ Marinating – This is a common process in Chinese and other Oriental cookery to add flavour to meat, fish and vegetables. The food is steeped in a mixture of flavours, which could include soy sauce, rice wine, garlic, ginger or spices. Marinating time is usually at least 20 minutes, but often can be as long as overnight. Food is usually removed from the marinade before cooking.

◦ Velveting – This is a particularly useful technique in Chinese cooking which helps to protect delicate foods, such as chicken breasts, from overcooking. The food is coated with a mixture of cornflour and egg white and sometimes salt. The mixture is marinated in the refrigerator for 20–30 minutes before cooking.

Cooking Techniques

❧ Thickening – There are two useful ways of thickening sauces. The first is to use cornflour mixed until smooth with a little water that is then whisked into the hot, not boiling, sauce. The sauce is brought up to the simmer and cooked gently for about 2 minutes until thickened. The other method of thickening is to reduce the sauce; the liquid is simmered until most of the excess liquid has boiled off, leaving a concentrated and thickened sauce.

❧ Blanching – This method involves cooking food in boiling water or moderately hot oil for a few minutes so that it is partly cooked, which speeds up the cooking process later on, so that other elements of the dish do not overcook. Chicken is often blanched in oil after velveting, meat is often blanched in water to remove excess fat and vegetables are often blanched in water, drained and refreshed under cold water, before being drained again and dried. In the case of vegetables, stir-frying merely heats them through and finishes the cooking.

❧ Braising – This is a method often applied to tougher cuts of meat that need long, slow cooking times to remain moist. The food is usually browned and then cooked in stock or liquid to which other flavourings are also added. The mixture is brought up to simmering point and then cooked gently until tender.

∾ Poaching – This is a method of cooking meat or fish in simmering liquid until nearly cooked so that it can be added to soup or combined with a sauce to finish the cooking.

∾ Slow-simmering and steeping – Slow-simmered food is cooked very gently in liquid that just simmers. Simmering is the method for making stock. Steeping is a similar method, except that the heat is turned off and the heat of the liquid alone finishes off the cooking process.

∾ Steaming – Steaming is an ancient technique currently enjoying a revival because it adds no fat to the food being cooked. Steamed foods are cooked on a gentle, moist heat. Steaming is particularly suited to vegetable and fish.

Woks can be used as steamers in two ways. The first method is described under the section on bamboo steamers. The second method involves putting about 5 cm/2 inches of water in a stable wok on the hob. A metal or wooden rack or trivet is then placed into the wok and the water is brought to the boil. The food to be steamed should be arranged on a plate and the plate should be lowered on to the rack. The wok then needs to be covered tightly with a lid. For longer cooking times, the water may need replenishing.

∾ Shallow-frying – This is similar to sautéing as it involves more oil than stir-frying, but less than deep-frying. Food is fried first on one side and then on the other. Often the excess oil is drained off and a sauce is made in the same pan. A frying pan is preferable for shallow-frying rather than a wok.

∾ Deep-frying – This is another very important technique in Far Eastern cookery. Woks are very useful for deep-frying as they use far less oil than conventional deep-fat fryers. Although a deep-fat fryer is safer, a few precautions mean that deep-frying in a wok is very easy. Ensure that the wok sits securely on the hob, either by using a flat-bottomed wok or a wok stand.

Carefully add the oil, ensuring that the wok is no more than half full. Heat up slowly to the required temperature.

To test for temperature, either use a thermo-meter made for the purpose or the following test. Add a small cube of crustless bread and time how long it takes to brown. Generally, if the bread browns in 30 seconds, the oil is at the correct temperature. If it browns more quickly the oil is too hot. If it takes longer to brown the oil is too cold. Allow the oil to return to the correct temperature between batches of food and do not overfill the wok. Do not leave the wok unsupervised on the stove when deep frying.

It is also important that food to be deep-fried is dry. Lift food from a marinade and blot thoroughly on kitchen paper. If using batter, allow any excess to drip off before adding to the oil.

Oil used for deep-frying can be reused. Allow the oil to cool completely and then strain into a clean jar or other container. Label the jar with the type of food the oil was used for and only reuse it for the same type of food. Oil can be reused up to 3 times.

- Stir-frying – This is the most famous of Asian cooking techniques and is used throughout China and the Far East as well as in India. It is possibly the most tricky of wok techniques because it involves a lot of preparation as well as a good source of heat. Its advantage is that stir-fried foods can be cooked very quickly in very little oil so that they retain their colour, flavour and texture. It is very important that stir-fried foods are not greasy or overcooked.

- Twice-cooking – As the name implies, this is a two-step process involving two different techniques, such as simmering and stir-frying. For example, pork ribs may be gently simmered to remove the excess fat before draining and stir-frying or braising with other flavours.

Stir-frying Steps

Once all the ingredients are prepared and to hand:

∞ Heat the wok or frying pan over the highest heat until it is very hot before adding the oil. This prevents the food from sticking and ensures an even heat. Add the oil and using a spatula or long-handled spoon, distribute it evenly over the surface. It should be very hot – almost smoking – before you add any ingredients (unless you are adding flavouring ingredients). If you are flavouring the oil, for example with garlic, ginger, spring onions or chilli (or a combination) do not let the oil become smoking hot because these types of ingredients will burn at such high temperatures and become bitter. Add to hot but not smoking oil and toss the ingredients around quickly for a few seconds. In some recipes these ingredients are removed and discarded.

∞ Now add the next ingredients as described in the recipe and proceed to stir-fry by tossing quickly in the wok using a spatula or long-handled spoon. When cooking meat, allow it to rest for a few seconds between stirring it. Otherwise keep the food moving, transferring it from the bottom to the sides of the wok and back again. Because of the high heat involved when stir-frying, there may be some spluttering and splattering of hot fat, so take care during this stage of cooking.

∞ Once everything is cooked, some stir-fried dishes are thickened with a mixture of cornflour and water. To avoid a lumpy sauce, make sure the mixture is smooth and reduce the heat to just below simmering point before adding it. Stir in the cornflour mixture then increase the heat to a simmer and cook for a further 2–3 minutes, until the sauce is thickened, smooth and coats all the ingredients.

Garnishes

Oriental cuisines pay a lot of attention to the finished appearance of food and this is one reason for cutting ingredients carefully. Often dishes will be garnished attractively with anything from simple shredded chillies to more elaborate spring onion tassels. Thai cooks often go to elaborate lengths, carving flowers from carrots or making tomato roses as garnishes. In fact, the Thai Royal family employs an official Fruit Carver (a hereditary post) for special occasions. The home cook can create some simple effects with everyday ingredients and a sharp knife.

∾ **Chilli Flowers** – Take a well-formed red chilli, about 5–7.5 cm/2–3 inches long, with the stem intact. Hold the chilli by the stem and, using a fine sharp knife, cut from the tip to the stem, at equal distances all the way around, without cutting through the stem. Try to leave the seeds intact. Gently pull back the strips and drop into iced water. The strips will curl back into a flower.

∾ **Spring Onion Tassels** – Trim the top green end of a spring onion and cut a piece about 5–7.5 cm/2–3 inches long, including about 1 cm/^{1}/$_2$ inch of the white base. With a fine, sharp knife, and holding the white part as a base, shred the green part as finely as possible. Drop into a bowl of iced water until the shreds curl back.

Hygiene in the Kitchen

It is well worth remembering that many foods can carry some form of bacteria. In most cases, the worst it will lead to is a bout of food poisoning or gastroenteritis, although for certain people this can be more serious. The risk can be reduced or eliminated by good food hygiene and proper cooking.

Do not buy food that is past its sell-by date and do not consume any food that is past its use-by date. When buying food, use your eyes and nose. If the food looks tired, limp or a bad colour or it has a rank, acrid or simply bad smell, do not buy or eat it under any circumstances. Do take special care when preparing raw meat and fish.

A separate chopping board should be used for each food; wash the knife, board and the hands thoroughly before handling or preparing any other food.

Regularly clean, defrost and clear out the refrigerator or freezer – it is worth checking the packaging to see exactly how long each product is safe to freeze.

Avoid handling food if suffering from an upset stomach, as bacteria can be passed on through food preparation.

Dish cloths and tea towels must be washed and changed regularly. Ideally, use disposable cloths which should be replaced on a daily basis. More durable cloths should be left to soak in bleach, then washed in the washing machine on a boil wash.

Keep the hands, cooking utensils and food preparation surfaces clean and do not allow pets to climb onto any work surfaces.

Buying

Avoid bulk buying where possible, especially fresh produce such as meat, poultry, fish, fruit and vegetables, unless buying for the freezer. Fresh foods lose their nutritional value rapidly, so buying a little at a time minimises loss of nutrients. It also eliminates a packed refrigerator, which reduces the effectiveness of the refrigeration process.

When buying prepackaged goods such as cans or pots of cream and yogurts, check that the packaging is intact and not damaged or pierced at all. Cans should not be dented, pierced or rusty. Check the sell-by dates even for cans and packets of dry ingredients such as flour and rice. Store fresh foods in the refrigerator as soon as possible – not in the car or the office.

When buying frozen foods, ensure that they are not heavily iced on the outside and the contents feel completely frozen. Ensure that the frozen foods have been stored in the cabinet at the correct storage level and the temperature is below -18°C/-0.4°F. Pack in cool bags to transport home and place in the freezer as soon as possible after purchase.

Preparation

Make sure that all work surfaces and utensils are clean and dry. Hygiene should be given priority at all times. Separate chopping boards should be used for raw and cooked meats, fish and

Hygiene in the Kitchen

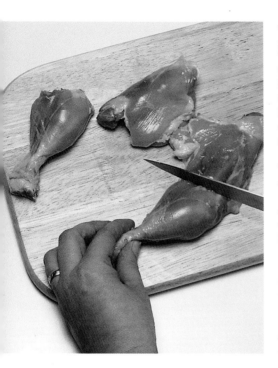

vegetables. Currently, a variety of good-quality plastic boards come in various designs and colours. This makes differentiating easier and the plastic has the added hygienic advantage of being washable at high temperatures in the dishwasher. (NB: If using the board for fish, first wash in cold water, then in hot, to prevent odour!) Also, remember that knives and utensils should always be thoroughly cleaned after use.

When cooking, be particularly careful to keep cooked and raw food separate to avoid any contamination. It is worth washing all fruits and vegetables, regardless of whether they are going to be eaten raw or lightly cooked. This rule should apply even to prewashed herbs and salads.

Do not reheat food more than once. If using a microwave, always check that the food is piping hot all the way through. In theory, the food should reach a minimum temperature of 70°C/158°F and needs to be cooked at that temperature for at least 3 minutes to ensure that any bacteria in the food are killed.

All poultry must be thoroughly thawed before using, including chicken and poussin. Remove the food to be thawed from the freezer and place in a shallow dish to contain the juices.

Leave the food in the refrigerator until it is completely thawed. A 1.4 kg/3 lb whole chicken will take about 26–30 hours to thaw. To speed up the process, immerse the chicken in cold water. However, make sure that the water is changed regularly. When the joints can move freely and no ice crystals remain in the cavity, the bird is completely thawed.

Once thawed, remove the wrapper and pat the chicken dry. Place the chicken in a shallow dish, cover lightly and store as close to the base of the refrigerator as possible. The chicken should be cooked as soon as possible.

Some foods can be cooked from frozen, including many prepacked foods such as soups, sauces, casseroles and breads. Where applicable, follow the manufacturers' instructions.

Vegetables and fruits can also be cooked from frozen, but meats and fish should be thawed first. The only time food can be refrozen is when the food has been thoroughly thawed, then cooked. Once the food has cooled, then it can be frozen again. On such occasions, the food can only be stored for one month.

All poultry and game (except for duck) must be cooked thoroughly. When cooked, the juices will run clear from the thickest part of the bird – the best area to try is usually the thigh. Other meats, such as minced meat and pork, should be cooked right the way through. Fish should turn opaque, be firm in texture and break easily into large flakes.

When cooking leftovers, make sure they are reheated until piping hot and that any sauce or soup reaches boiling point first.

Storing, Refrigerating and Freezing

Meat, poultry, fish, seafood and dairy products should all be refrigerated. The temperature of the refrigerator should be between 1–5°C/34–41°F, while the freezer temperature should not rise above -18°C/-0.4°F.

To ensure the optimum refrigerator and freezer temperature, avoid leaving the door open for a long time. Try not to overstock the refrigerator, as this reduces the airflow inside and affects the efficiency in cooling the food within. When refrigerating cooked food, allow it to cool down quickly and completely before refrigerating. Hot food will raise the temperature of the refrigerator and possibly affect or spoil other food stored in it.

Food within the refrigerator and freezer should always be covered. Raw and cooked food should be stored in separate parts of the refrigerator. Cooked food should be kept on the top shelves of the refrigerator, while raw meat, poultry and fish should be placed on bottom shelves to avoid drips and cross contamination.

It is recommended that eggs should be refrigerated in order to maintain their freshness and shelf life.

Take care that frozen foods are not stored in the freezer for too long. Blanched vegetables can be stored for one month; beef, lamb, poultry and pork for six months; and unblanched vegetables and fruits in syrup for a year. Oily fish and sausages can be stored for three months. Dairy products can last four to six months, while cakes and pastries can be kept in the freezer for three to six months.

High-risk Foods

Certain foods may carry risks to people who are considered vulnerable, such as the elderly, the ill, pregnant women, babies, young infants and those suffering from a recurring illness. It is advisable to avoid those foods listed below, which belong to a higher-risk category.

There is a slight chance that some eggs carry the bacteria salmonella. Cook the eggs until both the yolk and the white are firm to eliminate this risk.

Pay particular attention to dishes and products incorporating lightly cooked or raw eggs, which should be eliminated from the diet. Sauces including Hollandaise, mayonnaise, mousses, soufflés and meringues all use raw or lightly cooked eggs, as do custard-based dishes, ice creams and sorbets. These are all considered high-risk foods to the vulnerable groups mentioned above.

Certain meats and poultry also carry the potential risk of salmonella and so should be cooked thoroughly until the juices run clear and there is no pinkness left. Unpasteurised products such as milk, cheese (especially soft cheese), pâté and meat (both raw and cooked) all have the potential risk of listeria and should be avoided.

When buying seafood, buy from a reputable source which has a high turnover to ensure freshness. Fish should have bright, clear eyes, shiny skin and bright pink or red gills. The fish should feel stiff to the touch, with a slight smell of sea air and iodine. The flesh of fish steaks and fillets should be translucent, with no signs of discolouration.

Molluscs such as scallops, clams and mussels are sold fresh and are still alive. Avoid any that are open or do not close when tapped lightly. In the same way, univalves such as cockles or winkles should withdraw back into their shells when lightly prodded. When choosing cephalopods such as squid and octopus, they should have a firm flesh and pleasant sea smell.

As with all fish, whether it is shellfish or wet fish, care is required when freezing it. It is imperative to check whether the fish has been frozen before. If it has been frozen, then it should not be frozen again under any circumstances.

Hygiene in the Kitchen

Finger Food

Quick, delicious and just small enough to justify trying a bit of everything, finger food is hard to beat. Covering a wide variety of flavours and textures from far flung countries, this section boasts the best finger food around. From bigger eats like the Falafel Sandwiches or flavour-filled Caribbean Empanadas, to smaller snacks such as Wok-fried Snacks and Onion Bhajis, your hands will be itching to get stuck in.

Hoisin Chicken Pancakes

Serves 4

3 tbsp hoisin sauce
1 garlic clove, peeled
and crushed
2.5 cm/1 inch piece root ginger,
peeled and finely grated
1 tbsp soy sauce
1 tsp sesame oil
salt and freshly ground
black pepper
4 skinless chicken thighs
$^{1}/_{2}$ cucumber, peeled (optional)
12 bought Chinese pancakes
6 spring onions, trimmed
and cut lengthways into
fine shreds
sweet chilli dipping sauce,
to serve

Preheat the oven to 190°C/ 375°F/Gas Mark 5. In a non-metallic bowl, mix the hoisin sauce with the garlic, ginger, soy sauce, sesame oil and seasoning.

Add the chicken thighs and turn to coat in the mixture. Cover loosely and leave in the refrigerator to marinate for 3–4 hours, turning the chicken from time to time.

Remove the chicken from the marinade and place in a roasting tin. Reserve the marinade. Bake in the preheated oven for 30 minutes basting occasionally with the marinade.

Cut the cucumber in half lengthways and remove the seeds by running a teaspoon down the middle to scoop them out. Cut into thin batons.

Place the pancakes in a steamer to warm or heat according to packet instructions. Thinly slice the hot chicken and arrange on a plate with the shredded spring onions, cucumber and pancakes.

Place a spoonful of the chicken in the middle of each warmed pancake and top with pieces of cucumber, spring onion, and a little dipping sauce. Roll up and serve immediately.

Moo Shi Pork

Serves 4

175 g/6 oz pork fillet
2 tsp Chinese rice wine or
dry sherry
2 tbsp light soy sauce
1 tsp cornflour
25 g/1 oz dried golden needles,
soaked and drained
2 tbsp groundnut oil
3 medium eggs, lightly beaten
1 tsp freshly grated root ginger
3 spring onions, trimmed and
thinly sliced
150 g/5 oz bamboo shoots,
cut into fine strips
salt and freshly ground
black pepper
8 mandarin pancakes, steamed
hoisin sauce
sprigs of fresh coriander,
to garnish

Cut the pork across the grain into 1 cm/1/2 inch slices, then cut into thin strips. Place in a bowl with the Chinese rice wine or sherry, soy sauce and cornflour. Mix well and reserve. Trim off the tough ends of the golden needles, then cut in half and reserve.

Heat a wok or large frying pan, add 1 tablespoon of the groundnut oil and when hot, add the lightly beaten eggs, and cook for 1 minute, stirring all the time, until scrambled. Remove and reserve. Wipe the wok clean with absorbent kitchen paper.

Return the wok to the heat, add the remaining oil and when hot transfer the pork strips from the marinade mixture to the wok, shaking off as much marinade as possible. Stir-fry for 30 seconds, then add the ginger, spring onions and bamboo shoots and pour in the marinade. Stir-fry for 2–3 minutes or until cooked.

Return the scrambled eggs to the wok, season to taste with salt and pepper and stir for a few seconds until mixed well and heated through. Divide the mixture between the pancakes, drizzle each with 1 teaspoon of hoisin sauce and roll up. Garnish and serve immediately.

Spicy Beef Pancakes

Serves 4

50 g/2 oz plain flour
pinch salt
$^1/_2$ tsp Chinese five spice powder
1 large egg yolk
150 ml/$^1/_4$ pint milk
4 tsp sunflower oil
slices of spring onion, to garnish

For the spicy beef filling:

1 tbsp sesame oil
4 spring onions, sliced
1 cm/$^1/_2$ inch piece fresh root
ginger, peeled and grated
1 garlic clove, peeled
and crushed
300 g/11 oz sirloin steak, trimmed
and cut into strips
1 red chilli, deseeded and
finely chopped
1 tsp sherry vinegar
1 tsp soft dark brown sugar
1 tbsp dark soy sauce

Sift the flour, salt and Chinese five spice powder into a bowl and make a well in the centre. Add the egg yolk and a little of the milk. Gradually beat in, drawing in the flour to make a smooth batter. Whisk in the rest of the milk.

Heat 1 teaspoon of the sunflower oil in a small heavy-based frying pan. Pour in just enough batter to thinly coat the base of the pan. Cook over a medium heat for 1 minute, or until the underside of the pancake is golden brown. Turn or toss the pancake and cook for 1 minute, or until the other side of the pancake is golden brown. Make 7 more pancakes with the remaining batter. Stack them on a warmed plate as you make them, with greaseproof paper between each pancake. Cover with tinfoil and keep warm in a low oven.

Make the filling. Heat a wok or large frying pan, add the sesame oil and when hot, add the spring onions, ginger and garlic and stir-fry for 1 minute. Add the beef strips, stir-fry for 3–4 minutes, then stir in the chilli, vinegar, sugar and soy sauce. Cook for 1 minute, then remove from the heat.

Spoon one-eighth of the filling over one half of each pancake. Fold the pancakes in half, then fold in half again. Garnish with a few slices of spring onion and serve immediately.

Crispy Pancake Rolls Ⓥ

Serves 4

250 g/9 oz plain flour
pinch salt
1 medium egg
4 tsp sunflower oil
2 tbsp light olive oil
2 cm/³/₄ inch piece fresh root
ginger, peeled and grated
1 garlic clove, peeled
and crushed
225 g/8 oz tofu, drained and cut
into small dice
2 tbsp soy sauce
1 tbsp dry sherry
175 g/6 oz button mushrooms,
wiped and chopped
1 celery stalk, trimmed and
finely chopped
2 spring onions, trimmed and
finely chopped
2 tbsp groundnut oil
fresh coriander sprig and sliced
spring onion, to garnish

Sift 225 g/8 oz of the flour with the salt into a large bowl, make a well in the centre and drop in the egg. Beat to form a smooth, thin batter, gradually adding 300 ml/¹/₂ pint of water and drawing in the flour from the sides of the bowl. Mix the remaining flour with 1–2 tablespoons of water to make a thick paste. Reserve.

Heat a little sunflower oil in a 20.5 cm/8 inch omelette or frying pan and pour in 2 tablespoons of the batter. Cook for 1–2 minutes, flip over and cook for a further 1–2 minutes, or until firm. Slide from the pan and keep warm. Make more pancakes with the remaining batter.

Heat a wok or large frying pan, add the olive oil and when hot, add the ginger, garlic and tofu, stir-fry for 30 seconds, then pour in the soy sauce and sherry. Add the mushrooms, celery and spring onions. Stir-fry for 1–2 minutes, then remove from the wok and leave to cool.

Place a little filling in the centre of each pancake. Brush the edges, with the flour paste, fold in the edges, then roll up into parcels. Heat the groundnut oil to 180°C/350°F in the wok. Fry the pancake rolls for 2–3 minutes or until golden. Serve immediately, garnished with chopped spring onions and a sprig of coriander.

Duck in Crispy Wonton Shells

Serves 4

2 x 175 g/6 oz duck breasts
2 tbsp Chinese five spice powder
2 tbsp Sichuan peppercorns
1 tsp whole black peppercorns
3 tbsp cumin seeds
5 tbsp sea salt
6 slices fresh root ginger
6 spring onions, roughly chopped
1 tbsp cornflour
1 litre/1³/₄ pints vegetable oil
for frying
16 wonton wrappers
5 cm/2 inch piece cucumber, cut
into fine strips
125 ml/4 fl oz hoisin sauce

Rinse the duck and dry thoroughly with absorbent kitchen paper. Place the Chinese five spice powder, peppercorns, cumin seeds and salt in a pestle and mortar and crush. Rub the spice mix all over the duck. Wrap in clingfilm and refrigerate for 24 hours.

Place a rack in the wok and pour in boiling water to a depth of 5 cm/ 2 inches. Place the duck breasts with the ginger slices and 3 chopped spring onions in a heatproof dish on top of the rack. Cover and steam for 40–50 minutes, or until the duck is cooked. Pour off any excess fat from time to time and add more water if necessary. Remove the duck and leave until cooled.

Dust the duck breasts with cornflour, shaking off the excess. Heat the wok, add the oil and, when almost smoking, deep-fry the duck for 8 minutes. Drain, then shred the meat into bite-sized pieces. Shred the remaining spring onions.

Reheat the oil until smoking. Working with 1 wonton at a time, insert two wooden skewers into each one, hold in a taco shape and lower into the oil. Hold in the oil until crisp and golden brown. Drain on absorbent kitchen paper. Repeat with the remaining wontons. Fill the wontons with the duck, topped with the spring onions, cucumber and hoisin sauce and serve immediately.

Beef Fajitas with Avocado Sauce

Serves 3–6

2 tbsp sunflower oil
450 g/1 lb beef fillet or rump steak,
trimmed and cut into thin strips
2 garlic cloves, peeled
and crushed
1 tsp ground cumin
$1/4$ tsp cayenne pepper
1 tbsp paprika
230 g can chopped tomatoes
215 g can red kidney
beans, drained
1 tbsp freshly chopped coriander
1 avocado, peeled, pitted
and chopped
1 shallot, peeled and chopped
1 large tomato, skinned,
deseeded and chopped
1 red chilli, diced
1 tbsp lemon juice
6 large flour tortilla pancakes
3–4 tbsp soured cream
green salad, to serve

Heat the wok, add the oil, then stir-fry the beef for 3–4 minutes. Add the garlic and spices and continue to cook for a further 2 minutes. Stir the tomatoes into the wok, bring to the boil, cover and simmer gently for 5 minutes.

Meanwhile, blend the kidney beans in a food processor until slightly broken up, then add to the wok. Continue to cook for a further 5 minutes, adding 2–3 tablespoons of water. The mixture should be thick and fairly dry. Stir in the chopped coriander.

Mix the chopped avocado, shallot, tomato, chilli and lemon juice together. Spoon into a serving dish and reserve.

When ready to serve, warm the tortillas and spread with a little soured cream. Place a spoonful of the beef mixture on top, followed by a spoonful of the avocado sauce, then roll up. Repeat until all the mixture is used up. Serve immediately with a green salad.

Chicken Wraps

Serves 4

For the stir-fried chicken:
4 skinless chicken breast fillets
finely grated zest and juice of 1 lime
1 tbsp caster sugar
2 tsp dried oregano
$^1/_2$ tsp ground cinnamon
$^1/_4$ tsp cayenne pepper
3 tbsp sunflower oil
2 onions, peeled and sliced
1 green, 1 red and 1 yellow pepper,
deseeded and sliced
salt and freshly ground black pepper

For the tortillas:
250 g/9 oz plain flour
pinch salt
$^1/_4$ tsp baking powder
50 g/2 oz white vegetable fat

To serve:
soured cream
guacamole

Slice the chicken across the grain into 2 cm/$^3/_4$ inch wide strips. Place in a bowl with the lime zest and juice, sugar, oregano, cinnamon and cayenne pepper. Mix well and leave to marinate while making the tortillas.

Sift the flour, salt and baking powder into a bowl. Rub in the white fat, then sprinkle over 4 tablespoons of warm water and mix to a stiff dough. Knead on a lightly floured surface for 10 minutes until smooth and elastic. Divide the dough into 12 equal pieces and roll out each to a 15 cm/6 inch circle. Cover with clingfilm to prevent them drying out before you cook them.

Heat a non-stick wok and cook each tortilla for about 1 minute on each side, or until golden and slightly blistered. Remove the tortillas and keep them warm and pliable in a clean tea towel.

Heat 2 tablespoons of the oil in the wok and stir-fry the onions for 5 minutes until lightly coloured. Remove with a slotted spoon and reserve.

Add the remaining oil to the wok and heat. Drain the chicken from the marinade and add it to the wok. Stir-fry for 5 minutes, then return the onions, add the pepper slices and cook for a further 3–4 minutes, or until the chicken is cooked through and the vegetables are tender. Season to taste with salt and pepper and serve immediately with the tortillas, soured cream and guacamole.

Coriander Chicken Cakes

Serves 4

1/4 cucumber, peeled
1 shallot, peeled and thinly sliced
6 radishes, trimmed and sliced
350 g/12 oz skinless boneless
chicken thigh
4 tbsp fresh coriander
roughly chopped
2 spring onions, trimmed and
roughly chopped
1 red chilli, deseeded
and chopped
finely grated rind of 1/2 lime
2 tbsp soy sauce
1 tbsp caster sugar
2 tbsp rice vinegar
1 red chilli, deseeded and
finely sliced
freshly chopped coriander,
to garnish

Preheat the oven to 190°C/375°F/Gas Mark 5. Halve the cucumber lengthwise, deseed and dice.

In a bowl mix the shallot and radishes. Chill until ready to serve with the diced cucumber.

Place the chicken thighs in a food processor and blend until coarsely chopped. Add the coriander and spring onions to the chicken with the chilli, lime rind and soy sauce. Blend again until mixed.

Using slightly damp hands, shape the chicken mixture into 12 small rounds. Place the rounds on a lightly oiled baking tray and bake in the preheated oven for 15 minutes, until golden.

In a small pan heat the sugar with 2 tablespoons of water until dissolved. Simmer until syrupy. Remove from the heat and allow to cool a little, then stir in the vinegar and chilli slices. Pour over the cucumber and the radish and shallot salad. Garnish with the chopped coriander and serve the chicken cakes with the salad immediately.

Honey ❀ Ginger Prawns

Serves 4

1 carrot
50 g/2 oz bamboo shoots
4 spring onions
1 tbsp clear honey
1 tbsp tomato ketchup
1 tsp soy sauce
2.5 cm/1 inch piece fresh root
ginger, peeled and
finely grated
1 garlic clove, peeled and crushed
1 tbsp lime juice
175 g/6 oz peeled prawns, thawed
if frozen
2 heads little gem
lettuce leaves
2 tbsp freshly chopped coriander
salt and freshly ground
black pepper

To garnish:

fresh coriander sprigs
lime slices

Cut the carrot into matchstick-size pieces, roughly chop the bamboo shoots and finely slice the spring onions. Combine the bamboo shoots with the carrot matchsticks and spring onions.

In a wok or large frying pan gently heat the honey, tomato ketchup, soy sauce, ginger, garlic and lime juice with 3 tablespoons of water. Bring to the boil. Add the carrot mixture and stir-fry for 2–3 minutes until the vegetables are hot.

Add the prawns and continue to stir-fry for 2 minutes. Remove the wok or frying pan from the heat and reserve until cooled slightly.

Divide the little gem lettuce into leaves and rinse lightly.

Stir the chopped coriander into the prawn mixture and season to taste with salt and pepper. Spoon into the lettuce leaves and serve immediately garnished with fresh coriander sprigs and lime slices.

Shredded Duck in Lettuce Leaves

Serves 4–6

15 g/¹/₂ oz dried Chinese
(shiitake) mushrooms
2 tbsp vegetable oil
400 g/14 oz boneless, skinless
duck breast, cut crossways
into thin strips
1 red chilli, deseeded and
diagonally thinly sliced
4–6 spring onions, trimmed and
diagonally sliced
2 garlic cloves, peeled
and crushed
75 g/3 oz beansprouts
3 tbsp soy sauce
1 tbsp Chinese rice wine or
dry sherry
1–2 tsp clear honey or
brown sugar
4–6 tbsp hoisin sauce
large, crisp lettuce leaves such as
iceberg or cos
handful of fresh mint leaves
dipping sauce

Cover the dried Chinese mushrooms with almost boiling water, leave for 20 minutes, then drain and slice thinly.

Heat a large wok, add the oil and when hot stir-fry the duck for 3–4 minutes, or until sealed. Remove with a slotted spoon and reserve.

Add the chilli, spring onions, garlic and Chinese mushrooms to the wok and stir-fry for 2–3 minutes, or until softened.

Add the beansprouts, the soy sauce, Chinese rice wine or dry sherry and honey or brown sugar to the wok, and continue to stir-fry for 1 minute, or until blended.

Stir in the reserved duck and stir-fry for 2 minutes, or until well mixed together and heated right through. Transfer to a heated serving dish.

Arrange the hoisin sauce in a small bowl on a tray or plate with a pile of lettuce leaves and the mint leaves.

Let each guest spoon a little hoisin sauce onto a lettuce leaf, then top with a large spoonful of the stir-fried duck and vegetables and roll up the leaf to enclose the filling. Serve with the dipping sauce.

Sweet Potato Crisps ❧ Mango Salsa Ⓥ

Serves 6

For the salsa:

1 large mango, peeled, stoned
and cut into small cubes
8 cherry tomatoes, quartered
$1/2$ cucumber, peeled if preferred
and finely diced
1 red onion, peeled and
finely chopped
pinch of sugar
1 red chilli, deseeded and
finely chopped
2 tbsp rice vinegar
2 tbsp olive oil
grated rind and juice of 1 lime

For the crisps:

450 g/1 lb sweet potatoes, peeled
and thinly sliced
vegetable oil, for deep frying
sea salt
2 tbsp freshly chopped mint

To make the salsa, mix the mango with the tomatoes, cucumber and onion. Add the sugar, chilli, vinegar, oil and the lime rind and juice. Mix together thoroughly, cover and leave for 45–50 minutes.

Soak the potatoes in cold water for 40 minutes to remove as much of the excess starch as possible. Drain and dry thoroughly in a clean tea towel, or absorbent kitchen paper.

Heat the oil to 190°C/375°F in a deep fryer. When at the correct temperature, place half the potatoes in the frying basket, then carefully lower the potatoes into the hot oil and cook for 4–5 minutes, or until they are golden brown, shaking the basket every minute so that they do not stick together.

Drain the potato crisps on absorbent kitchen paper, sprinkle with sea salt and place under a preheated moderate grill for a few seconds to dry out. Repeat with the remaining potatoes. Stir the mint into the salsa and serve with the potato crisps.

Potato Skins

4 large baking potatoes
2 tbsp olive oil
2 tsp paprika
125 g/4 oz pancetta, roughly chopped
6 tbsp double cream
125 g/4 oz Gorgonzola cheese
1 tbsp freshly chopped parsley

To serve:

reduced-calorie mayonnaise
sweet chilli dipping sauce
tossed green salad

Preheat the oven to 200°C/ 400°F/Gas Mark 6. Scrub the potatoes, then prick a few times with a fork or skewer and place directly on the top shelf of the oven. Bake in the preheated oven for at least 1 hour, or until tender. The potatoes are cooked when they yield gently to the pressure of your hand.

Set the potatoes aside until cool enough to handle, then cut in half and scoop the flesh into a bowl and reserve. Preheat the grill and line the grill rack with tinfoil.

Mix together the oil and the paprika and use half to brush the outside of the potato skins. Place on the grill rack under the preheated hot grill and cook for 5 minutes, or until crisp, turning as necessary.

Heat the remaining paprika-flavoured oil and gently fry the pancetta until crisp. Add to the potato flesh along with the cream, Gorgonzola cheese and parsley. Halve the potato skins and fill with the Gorgonzola filling. Return to the oven for a further 15 minutes to heat through. Sprinkle with a little more paprika and serve immediately with mayonnaise, sweet chilli sauce and a green salad.

Thai Crab Cakes

ℭ

Serves 4

200 g/7 oz easy-cook basmati rice
450 ml/³/₄ pint chicken stock, heated
200 g/7 oz cooked crab meat
125 g/4 oz cod fillet, skinned and minced
5 spring onions, trimmed and finely chopped
1 lemon grass stalk, outer leaves discarded and finely chopped
1 green chilli, deseeded and finely chopped
1 tbsp freshly grated root ginger
1 tbsp freshly chopped coriander
1 tbsp plain flour
1 medium egg
salt and freshly ground black pepper
2 tbsp vegetable oil, for frying

To serve:

sweet chilli dipping sauce
fresh salad leaves

Put the rice in a large saucepan and add the hot stock. Bring to the boil, cover and simmer over a low heat, without stirring, for 18 minutes, or until the grains are tender and all the liquid is absorbed.

To make the cakes, place the crab meat, fish, spring onions, lemon grass, chilli, ginger, coriander, flour and egg in a food processor. Blend until all the ingredients are mixed thoroughly, then season to taste with salt and pepper. Add the rice to the processor and blend once more, but do not over mix.

Remove the mixture from the processor and place on a clean work surface. With damp hands, divide into 12 even-sized patties. Transfer to a plate, cover and chill in the refrigerator for about 30 minutes.

Heat the oil in a heavy-based frying pan and cook the crab cakes, 4 at a time, for 3–5 minutes on each side until crisp and golden. Drain on absorbent kitchen paper and serve immediately with a chilli dipping sauce.

Barbecued Fish Kebabs

Serves 4

For the kebabs:

450 g/1 lb herring
or mackerel fillets, cut
into chunks
2 small red onions, peeled
and quartered
16 cherry tomatoes
salt and freshly ground
black pepper

For the sauce:

150 ml /¹/₄ pint fish stock
5 tbsp tomato ketchup
2 tbsp Worcestershire sauce
2 tbsp wine vinegar
2 tbsp brown sugar
2 drops Tabasco
2 tbsp tomato purée

Line a grill rack with a single layer of tinfoil and preheat the grill at a high temperature, 2 minutes before use.

If using wooden skewers, soak in cold water for 30 minutes to prevent them from catching alight during cooking.

Meanwhile, prepare the sauce. Add the fish stock, tomato ketchup, Worcestershire sauce, vinegar, sugar, Tabasco and tomato purée to a small saucepan. Stir well and leave to simmer for 5 minutes.

When ready to cook, drain the skewers, if necessary, then thread the fish chunks, the quartered red onions and the cherry tomatoes alternately on to the skewers.

Season the kebabs to taste with salt and pepper and brush with the sauce. Grill under the preheated grill for 8–10 minutes, basting with the sauce occasionally during cooking. Turn the kebabs often to ensure that they are cooked thoroughly and evenly on all sides. Serve immediately with couscous.

Citrus Monkfish Kebabs

Serves 4

For the marinade:

1 tbsp sunflower oil
finely grated rind and juice
of 1 lime
1 tbsp lemon juice
1 sprig of freshly
chopped rosemary
1 tbsp whole-grain mustard
1 garlic clove, peeled
and crushed
salt and freshly ground
black pepper

For the kebabs:

450 g/1 lb monkfish tail
8 raw tiger prawns
1 small green courgette, trimmed
and sliced
4 tbsp of half-fat crème fraîche

Preheat the grill and line the grill rack with tinfoil. Mix all the marinade ingredients together in a small bowl and reserve.

Using a sharp knife, cut down both sides of the monkfish tail. Remove the bone and discard. Cut away and discard any skin, then cut the monkfish into bite-sized cubes. Peel the prawns, leaving the tails intact and remove the thin black vein that runs down the back of each prawn. Place the fish and prawns in a shallow dish.

Pour the marinade over the fish and prawns. Cover lightly and leave to marinate in the refrigerator for 30 minutes. Spoon the marinade over the fish and prawns occasionally during this time. Soak the skewers in cold water for 30 minutes, then drain.

Thread the cubes of fish, prawns and courgettes on to the drained skewers. Arrange on the grill rack then place under the preheated grill and cook for 5–7 minutes, or until cooked thoroughly and the prawns have turned pink. Occasionally brush with the remaining marinade and turn the kebabs during cooking.

Mix 2 tablespoons of the marinade with the crème fraîche and serve as a dip with the kebabs.

Curried Prawn Kebabs

Serves 4–6

1 tbsp vegetable oil
1 tsp fennel seeds
1 tsp cumin seeds
1 tsp turmeric
1 tsp chilli powder
1 tsp ground coriander
1 red chilli, deseeded and chopped
5 cm/2 inch piece fresh root ginger, peeled and grated
2 tbsp lime juice
300 ml/$\frac{1}{2}$ pint natural yogurt
350 g/12 oz raw large prawns, peeled
2–3 limes, cut into wedges
salad and Indian-style bread, to serve
4–8 wooden kebab skewers, soaked in cold water for 30 minutes

Heat the oil in a wok or frying pan, add the seeds and fry for 30 seconds, or until they pop. Add the turmeric, chilli powder, ground coriander, chopped chilli and grated ginger and fry over a gentle heat for 2 minutes. Stir in the lime juice and cook, stirring, for 30 seconds. Remove from the heat and cool slightly before stirring in the yogurt.

Rinse the prawns and pat dry with absorbent kitchen paper, then place in a shallow dish large enough for the prawns to lie in a single layer. Pour the spicy yogurt over the prawns, cover lightly and leave to marinate in the refrigerator for at least 30 minutes, turning the prawns over a couple of times.

Line a grill rack with foil and preheat the grill, or light the barbecue. Drain the prawns, reserving the marinade, and thread them with the lime wedges onto the drained kebab skewers. Place on the grill rack or barbecue rack and cook for 5–10 minutes, or until cooked, turning the prawns over occasionally and brushing with a little of the reserved marinade. Turn the heat down if the prawns under the grill are cooking too quickly and beginning to burn. Serve with salad and bread.

Mixed Satay Sticks

Serves 4

12 large raw prawns
350 g/12 oz beef rump steak
1 tbsp lemon juice
1 garlic clove, peeled and crushed
pinch salt
2 tsp soft dark brown sugar
1 tsp ground cumin
1 tsp ground coriander
$1/4$ tsp ground turmeric
1 tbsp groundnut oil
fresh coriander leaves, to garnish

For the spicy peanut sauce:

1 shallot, peeled and very finely chopped
1 tsp demerara sugar
50 g/2 oz creamed coconut, chopped
pinch chilli powder
1 tbsp dark soy sauce
125 g/4 oz crunchy peanut butter

Preheat the grill to high just before required. Soak eight bamboo skewers in cold water for at least 30 minutes. Peel the prawns, leaving the tails on. Using a sharp knife, remove the black vein along the back of the prawns. Cut the beef into 1 cm/$1/2$ inch wide strips. Place the prawns and beef in separate bowls and sprinkle with the lemon juice.

Mix together the garlic, pinch salt, sugar, cumin, coriander, turmeric and groundnut oil to make a paste. Lightly brush over the prawns and beef. Cover and place in the refrigerator to marinate for at least 30 minutes, but for longer if possible.

Meanwhile, make the sauce. Pour 125 ml/4 fl oz of water into a small saucepan, add the shallot and sugar and heat gently until the sugar has dissolved. Stir in the creamed coconut and chilli powder. When melted, remove from the heat and stir in the peanut butter. Leave to cool slightly, then spoon into a serving dish.

Thread 3 prawns on to each of the four skewers and divide the sliced beef between the remaining skewers. Cook under the preheated grill for 4–5 minutes, turning occasionally. The prawns should be opaque and pink and the beef browned on the outside, but still pink in the centre. Transfer to warmed individual serving plates, garnish with a few fresh coriander leaves and serve immediately with the warm peanut sauce.

Chicken & Lamb Satay

Makes 16

225 g/8 oz skinless, boneless chicken breasts
225 g/8 oz lean lamb

For the marinade:
1 onion, peeled and finely chopped
2 garlic cloves, peeled and crushed
2.5 cm/1 inch piece fresh root ginger, peeled and grated
4 tbsp soy sauce
1 tsp ground coriander
2 tsp dark brown sugar
2 tbsp lime juice; 1 tbsp vegetable oil

For the peanut sauce:
300 ml/½ pint coconut milk
4 tbsp crunchy peanut butter
1 tbsp Thai fish sauce; 1 tsp lime juice
1 tbsp chilli powder
1 tbsp brown sugar
salt and freshly ground black pepper

coriander sprigs and lime wedges, to garnish

Preheat the grill just before cooking. Soak the bamboo skewers for 30 minutes before required. Cut the chicken and lamb into thin strips, about 7.5 cm/3 inches long and place in two shallow dishes.

Blend all the marinade ingredients together, then pour half over the chicken and half over the lamb. Stir until lightly coated, then cover with clingfilm and leave to marinate in the refrigerator for at least 2 hours, turning occasionally.

Remove the chicken and lamb from the marinade and thread on to the skewers. Reserve the marinade. Cook under the preheated grill for 8–10 minutes or until cooked, turning and brushing with the marinade.

Meanwhile, make the peanut sauce. Blend the coconut milk with the peanut butter, fish sauce, lime juice, chilli powder and sugar. Pour into a saucepan and cook gently for 5 minutes, stirring occasionally, then season to taste with salt and pepper. Garnish with coriander sprigs and lime wedges and serve the satays with the prepared sauce.

Marinated Vegetable Kebabs Ⓥ

Serves 4

2 small courgettes, cut into
2 cm/³/₄ inch pieces
¹/₂ green pepper, deseeded and
cut into 2.5 cm/1 inch pieces
¹/₂ red pepper, deseeded and cut
into 2.5 cm /1 inch pieces
¹/₂ yellow pepper, deseeded and
cut into 2.5 cm/1 inch pieces
8 baby onions, peeled
8 button mushrooms
8 cherry tomatoes
freshly chopped parsley, to garnish
freshly cooked couscous, to serve

Marinade:

1 tbsp light olive oil
4 tbsp dry sherry
2 tbsp light soy sauce
1 red chilli, deseeded and
finely chopped
2 garlic cloves, peeled and crushed
2.5 cm/1 inch piece root ginger,
peeled and finely grated

Place the courgettes, peppers and baby onions in a pan of just boiled water. Bring back to the boil and simmer for about 30 seconds.

Drain and rinse the cooked vegetables in cold water and dry on absorbent kitchen paper.

Thread the cooked vegetables and the mushrooms and tomatoes alternately on to skewers and place in a large shallow dish.

Make the marinade by whisking all the ingredients together until thoroughly blended. Pour the marinade evenly over the kebabs, then chill in the refrigerator for at least 1 hour. Spoon the marinade over the kebabs occasionally during this time.

Place the kebabs in a hot griddle pan or on a hot barbecue and cook gently for 10–12 minutes. Turn the kebabs frequently and brush with the marinade when needed. When the vegetables are tender, sprinkle over the chopped parsley and serve immediately with couscous.

Falafel Sandwiches Ⓥ

Serves 4

200 g/7 oz dried chickpeas, or
400 g can chickpeas
1 large onion, chopped
2 cloves garlic, chopped
3 tbsp fresh parsley, chopped
1 tsp ground coriander
1 tsp cumin
2 tbsp plain flour
salt and freshly
ground black pepper
vegetable oil, for frying
4 pitta breads
salad (such as lettuce,
tomatoes, cucumber, bean
sprouts), chopped or sliced
ready-made houmous

If using dried chickpeas, place in a bowl and cover with cold water. Allow to soak overnight.

Drain the chickpeas, place in a saucepan with fresh water, and bring to the boil. Allow to boil for 5 minutes, then lower the heat and simmer for about an hour. Drain and leave to cool for 15 minutes.

Combine the chickpeas, garlic, onion, ground coriander, cumin, salt and pepper (to taste) in a medium bowl. Add the flour. Either by hand or in a food processor, mash the mixture together, ensuring everything is well mixed, until you achieve a thick paste.

Roll the mixture into small balls, about the size of a ping pong ball. Flatten slightly with the palm of your hand.

Heat 5 cm/2 inches of oil in a large pan to 180°C/350°F and fry the patties for 5–7 minutes, until golden brown. Using a slotted spoon, remove and drain on absorbent kitchen paper.

Toast or grill the pitta breads lightly, split open and fill with salad, houmous and the falafel patties. Serve immediately.

Cheesy Chicken Burgers

Serves 6

1 tbsp sunflower oil; 1 small onion, peeled and finely chopped; 1 garlic clove, peeled and crushed; $1/2$ red pepper, deseeded and finely chopped; 450 g/1 lb fresh chicken mince; 2 tbsp 0%-fat Greek yogurt; 50 g/2 oz fresh brown breadcrumbs; 1 tbsp freshly chopped herbs, such as parsley or tarragon; 50 g/2 oz Cheshire cheese, crumbled; salt and freshly ground black pepper

For the relish:

200 g can sweetcorn, drained; 1 carrot, peeled, grated; $1/2$ green chilli, deseeded and finely chopped; 2 tsp cider vinegar; 2 tsp light soft brown sugar

To serve:

wholemeal or granary rolls; lettuce; sliced tomatoes; mixed salad leaves

Preheat the grill. Heat the oil in a frying pan and gently cook the onion and garlic for 5 minutes. Add the red pepper and cook for 5 minutes. Transfer into a mixing bowl and reserve.

Add the chicken, yogurt, breadcrumbs, herbs and cheese and season to taste with salt and pepper. Mix well. Divide the mixture equally into 6 and shape into burgers. Cover and chill in the refrigerator for at least 20 minutes.

To make the relish, put all the ingredients in a small saucepan with 1 tablespoon of water and heat gently, stirring occasionally until all the sugar has dissolved. Cover and cook over a low heat for 2 minutes, then uncover and cook for a further minute, or until the relish is thick.

Place the burgers on a lightly oiled grill pan and grill under a medium heat for 8–10 minutes on each side, or until browned and completely cooked through.

Warm the rolls if liked, then split in half and fill with the burgers, lettuce, sliced tomatoes and the prepared relish. Serve immediately with the salad leaves.

Aduki Bean ❧ Rice Burgers Ⓥ

Serves 4

2¹/₂ tbsp sunflower oil
1 medium onion, peeled and very
finely chopped
1 garlic clove, peeled and crushed
1 tsp curry paste
225 g/8 oz basmati rice
400 g can aduki beans, drained
and rinsed
225 ml/8 fl oz vegetable stock
125 g/4 oz firm tofu, crumbled
1 tsp garam masala
2 tbsp freshly chopped coriander
salt and freshly ground black pepper

For the carrot raita:
2 large carrots, peeled and grated
¹/₂ cucumber, cut into tiny dice
150 ml/¹/₄ pint Greek yogurt

To serve:
wholemeal baps
tomato slices
lettuce leaves

Heat 1 tablespoon of the oil in a saucepan and gently cook the onion for 10 minutes until soft. Add the garlic and curry paste and cook for a few more seconds. Stir in the rice and beans.

Pour in the stock, bring to the boil and simmer for 12 minutes, or until all the stock has been absorbed – do not lift the lid for the first 10 minutes of cooking. Reserve.

Lightly mash the tofu. Add to the rice mixture with the garam masala, coriander, salt and pepper. Mix.

Divide the mixture into 8 and shape into burgers. Chill in the refrigerator for 30 minutes.

Meanwhile, make the raita. Mix together the carrots, cucumber and Greek yogurt. Spoon into a small bowl and chill in the refrigerator until ready to serve.

Heat the remaining oil in a large frying pan. Fry the burgers, in batches if necessary, for 4–5 minutes on each side, or until lightly browned. Serve in the baps with tomato slices and lettuce. Accompany with the raita.

Vegetable ❧ Goats' Cheese Pizza Ⓥ

Serves 4

125 g/4 oz baking potato
1 tbsp olive oil
225 g/8 oz strong white flour
$^{1}/_{2}$ tsp salt
1 tsp easy-blend dried yeast

For the topping:

1 medium aubergine, thinly sliced
2 small courgettes, trimmed and
sliced lengthways
1 yellow pepper, quartered
and deseeded
1 red onion, peeled and sliced into
very thin wedges
5 tbsp olive oil
175 g/6 oz cooked new
potatoes, halved
400 g can chopped
tomatoes, drained
2 tsp freshly chopped oregano
125 g/4 oz mozzarella cheese, cut
into small cubes
125 g/4 oz goats' cheese, crumbled

Preheat the oven to 220°C/ 425°F/Gas Mark 7, 15 minutes before baking. Put a baking sheet in the oven to heat up. Cook the potato in lightly salted boiling water until tender. Peel and mash with the olive oil until smooth.

Sift the flour and salt into a bowl. Stir in the yeast. Add the mashed potato and 150 ml/$^{1}/_{4}$ pint warm water and mix to a soft dough. Knead for 5–6 minutes, until smooth. Put the dough in a bowl, cover with clingfilm and leave to rise in a warm place for 30 minutes.

To make the topping, arrange the aubergine, courgettes, pepper and onion, skin-side up, on a grill rack and brush with 4 tablespoons of the oil. Grill for 4–5 minutes. Turn the vegetables and brush with the remaining oil. Grill for 3–4 minutes. Cool, skin and slice the pepper. Put all of the vegetables in a bowl, add the halved new potatoes and toss gently together. Set aside.

Briefly re-knead the dough then roll out to a 30.5–35.5 cm/12–14 inch round, according to preferred thickness. Mix the tomatoes and oregano together and spread over the pizza base. Scatter over the mozzarella cheese. Put the pizza on the preheated baking sheet and bake for 8 minutes. Arrange the vegetables and goats' cheese on top and bake for 8–10 minutes. Serve.

Spinach ❧ Pine Nut Pizza Ⓥ

🍃

Serves 2–4

Basic pizza dough:

225 g/8 oz strong plain flour
$^1/_2$ tsp salt
$^1/_4$ tsp quick-acting dried yeast
150 ml/$^1/_4$ pint warm water
1 tbsp extra-virgin olive oil

For the topping:

3 tbsp olive oil
1 large red onion, peeled
and chopped
2 garlic cloves, peeled and
finely sliced
450 g/1 lb frozen spinach, thawed
and drained
salt and freshly ground
black pepper
3 tbsp passata
125 g/4 oz mascarpone cheese
1 tbsp toasted pine nuts

Preheat the oven to 220°C/ 425°F/ Gas Mark 7. Sift the flour and salt into a bowl and stir in the yeast. Make a well in the centre and gradually add the water and oil to form soft dough. Knead the dough on a floured surface for about 5 minutes until smooth and elastic. Place in a lightly oiled bowl and cover with clingfilm. Leave to rise in a warm place for 1 hour.

Knock the pizza dough with your fist a few times, shape and roll out thinly on a lightly floured board. Place on a lightly floured baking sheet and lift the edge to make a little rim. Place another baking sheet into the preheated oven to heat up.

Heat half the oil in a frying pan and gently fry the onion and garlic until soft and starting to change colour.

Squeeze out any excess water from the spinach and finely chop. Add to the onion and garlic with the remaining olive oil. Season to taste with salt and pepper.

Spread the passata on the pizza dough and top with the spinach mixture. Mix the mascarpone with the pine nuts and dot over the pizza. Slide the pizza on to the hot baking sheet and bake for 15–20 minutes. Transfer to a large plate and serve immediately.

Three Tomato Pizza Ⓥ

Serves 2–4

1 quantity pizza dough
(*see* page 92)
3 plum tomatoes
8 cherry tomatoes
6 sun-dried tomatoes
pinch sea salt
1 tbsp freshly chopped basil
2 tbsp extra-virgin olive oil
125 g/4 oz buffalo mozzarella
cheese (or vegetarian
mozzarella), sliced
freshly ground black pepper
fresh basil leaves, to garnish

Preheat the oven to 220°C/ 425°F/Gas Mark 7. Place a baking sheet into the oven to heat up.

Divide the prepared pizza dough into four equal pieces. Roll out one quarter of the pizza dough on a lightly floured board to form a 20.5 cm/8 inch round. Lightly cover the three remaining pieces of dough with clingfilm.

Roll out the other three pieces into rounds, one at a time. While rolling out any piece of dough, keep the others covered with the clingfilm.

Slice the plum tomatoes, halve the cherry tomatoes and chop the sun-dried tomatoes into small pieces. Place a few pieces of each type of tomato on each pizza base then season to taste with the sea salt.

Sprinkle with the chopped basil and drizzle with the olive oil. Place a few slices of mozzarella on each pizza and season with black pepper. Transfer the pizzas on to the heated baking sheet and cook for 15–20 minutes, or until the cheese is golden brown and bubbling. Garnish with the basil leaves and serve immediately.

Chilli Beef Calzone

Serves 4

1 quantity pizza dough
(*see* page 92)
1 tbsp sunflower oil
1 onion, peeled and
finely chopped
1 green pepper, deseeded
and chopped
225 g/8 oz minced beef steak
420 g can chilli beans
220 g can chopped tomatoes
mixed salad leaves, to serve

Preheat the oven to 220°C/ 425°F/ Gas Mark 7, 15 minutes before baking. Heat the oil in a large saucepan and gently cook the onion and pepper for 5 minutes.

Add the minced beef to the saucepan and cook for 10 minutes, until browned.

Add the chilli beans and tomatoes and simmer gently for 30 minutes, or until the mince is tender. Place a baking sheet into the preheated oven to heat up.

Divide the pizza dough into four equal pieces. Cover three pieces of the dough with clingfilm and roll out the other piece on a lightly floured board to a 20.5 cm/8 inch round.

Spoon a quarter of the chilli mixture on to half of the dough round and dampen the edges with a little water. Fold over the empty half of the dough and press the edges together well to seal.

Repeat this process with the remaining dough. Place on the hot baking sheet and bake for 15 minutes. Serve with the salad leaves.

Panzerotti Ⓥ

Makes 16

450 g/1 lb strong white flour
pinch salt
1 tsp easy-blend dried yeast
2 tbsp olive oil
300 ml/¹/₂ pint warm water
fresh rocket leaves, to serve

For the filling:

1 tbsp olive oil
1 small red onion, peeled and
finely chopped
2 garlic cloves, peeled and crushed
¹/₂ yellow pepper, deseeded
and chopped
1 small courgette, about 75 g/
3 oz, trimmed and chopped
50 g/2 oz black olives, pitted
and quartered
125 g/4 oz mozzarella cheese (or
vegetarian mozzarella), cubed
salt and freshly ground black pepper
5–6 tbsp tomato purée
1 tsp dried mixed herbs
oil for deep-frying

Sift the flour and salt into a bowl. Stir in the yeast. Make a well in the centre. Add the oil and the warm water and mix to a soft dough. Knead on a lightly floured surface until smooth and elastic. Put in an oiled bowl, cover and leave in a warm place to rise while making the filling.

To make the filling, heat the oil in a frying pan and cook the onion for 5 minutes. Add the garlic, yellow pepper and courgette. Cook for about 5 minutes, or until the vegetables are tender. Tip into a bowl and leave to cool slightly. Stir in the olives, mozzarella cheese and season to taste with salt and pepper.

Briefly reknead the dough. Divide into 16 equal pieces. Roll out each to a circle about 10 cm/4 inches. Mix together the tomato purée and dried herbs, then spread about 1 teaspoon on each circle, leaving a 2 cm/ ³/₄ inch border around the edge.

Divide the filling equally between the circles, it will seem a small amount, but if you overfill, they will leak during cooking. Brush the edges with water, then fold in half to enclose the filling. Press to seal, then crimp the edges.

Heat the oil in a deep-fat fryer to 180°C/350°F. Deep-fry the panzerotti in batches for 3 minutes, or until golden. Drain on absorbent kitchen paper and keep warm in a low oven until ready to serve with fresh rocket.

Caribbean Empanadas

Serves 4-6

175 g/6 oz lean fresh beef mince
175 g/6 oz lean fresh pork mince
1 onion, peeled and finely chopped
1 Scotch bonnet chilli, deseeded
and finely chopped
1 small red pepper, deseeded and
finely chopped
$^1/_2$ tsp ground cloves
1 tsp ground cinnamon
$^1/_2$ tsp ground allspice
1 tsp sugar
1 tbsp tomato purée
6 tbsp water
700 g/1$^1/_2$ lb prepared
shortcrust pastry
vegetable oil, for deep-frying
fresh herbs, to garnish
mango chutney (*see* page 142)

Place the mince in a nonstick frying pan and cook, stirring,
for 5–8 minutes, or until sealed. Break up any lumps with
a wooden spoon. Add the onion, chilli and red pepper together
with the spices and cook, stirring, for 10 minutes, or until the
onion has softened. Sprinkle in the sugar.

Blend the tomato purée with the water and stir into the meat.
Bring to the boil, then reduce the heat and simmer for
10 minutes. Allow to cool.

Roll the pastry out on a lightly floured surface and cut into
10 cm/4 inch rounds. Place a spoonful of the meat mixture onto
the centre of each pastry round and brush the edges with water.
Fold over, encasing the filling to form small pasties.

Heat the oil to a temperature of 180°C/350°F and deep-fry the
empanadas in batches, about 3 or 4 at a time, for 3–4 minutes,
or until golden. Drain on absorbent kitchen paper. Garnish and
serve with the mango relish.

Fried Whitebait

Serves 4

450 g/1 lb whitebait, fresh or frozen
oil, for frying
85 g/3 oz plain flour
$1/2$ tsp of cayenne pepper
salt and freshly ground black pepper

For the salad:

125 g/4 oz rocket leaves
125 g/4 oz cherry tomatoes, halved
75 g/3 oz cucumber, cut into dice
3 tbsp olive oil
1 tbsp fresh lemon juice
$1/2$ tsp Dijon mustard
$1/2$ tsp caster sugar

If the whitebait are frozen, thaw completely, then wipe dry with absorbent kitchen paper.

Start to heat the oil in a deep-fat fryer. Arrange the fish in a large, shallow dish and toss well in the flour, cayenne pepper and salt and pepper.

Deep fry the fish in batches for 2–3 minutes, or until crisp and golden. Keep the cooked fish warm while deep frying the remaining fish.

Meanwhile, to make the salad, arrange the rocket leaves, cherry tomatoes and cucumber on individual serving dishes. Whisk the olive oil and the remaining ingredients together and season lightly. Drizzle the dressing over the salad and serve with the whitebait.

Sweetcorn Fritters (V)

Serves 4

4 tbsp groundnut oil
1 small onion, peeled and
finely chopped
1 red chilli, deseeded and
finely chopped
1 garlic clove, peeled
and crushed
1 tsp ground coriander
325 g can sweetcorn
6 spring onions, trimmed and
finely sliced
1 medium egg, lightly beaten
salt and freshly ground
black pepper
3 tbsp plain flour
1 tsp baking powder
spring onion curls, to garnish
Thai-style chutney, to serve

Heat 1 tablespoon of the groundnut oil in a frying pan, add the onion and cook gently for 7–8 minutes or until beginning to soften. Add the chilli, garlic and ground coriander and cook for 1 minute, stirring continuously. Remove from the heat.

Drain the sweetcorn and tip into a mixing bowl. Lightly mash with a potato masher to break down the corn a little. Add the cooked onion mixture to the bowl with the spring onions and beaten egg. Season to taste with salt and pepper, then stir to mix together. Sift the flour and baking powder over the mixture and stir in.

Heat 2 tablespoons of the groundnut oil in a large frying pan. Drop 4 or 5 heaped teaspoonfuls of the sweetcorn mixture into the pan, and using a fish slice or spatula, flatten each to make a 1 cm/1⁄2 inch thick fritter.

Fry the fritters for 3 minutes, or until golden brown on the underside, turn over and fry for a further 3 minutes, or until cooked through and crisp.

Remove the fritters from the pan and drain on absorbent kitchen paper. Keep warm while cooking the remaining fritters, adding a little more oil if needed. Garnish with spring onion curls and serve immediately with a Thai-style chutney.

Sweet & Sour Battered Fish

Serves 4–6

450 g/1 lb cod fillet, skinned
150 g/5 oz plain flour
salt and freshly ground
black pepper
2 tbsp cornflour
2 tbsp arrowroot
vegetable oil for deep-frying

For the sweet-&-sour sauce:

4 tbsp orange juice
2 tbsp white wine vinegar
2 tbsp dry sherry
1 tbsp dark soy sauce
1 tbsp soft light brown sugar
2 tsp tomato purée
1 red pepper, deseeded and diced
2 tsp cornflour

Cut the fish into pieces about 5 cm x 2.5 cm/2 x 1 inch. Place 4 tablespoons of the flour in a small bowl, season with salt and pepper to taste, then add the fish strips a few at a time and toss until coated.

Sift the remaining flour into a bowl with a pinch salt, the cornflour and arrowroot. Gradually whisk in 300 ml/$^1/_2$ pint iced water to make a smooth, thin batter.

Heat the oil in a wok or deep-fat fryer to 190˚C/ 375˚F. Working in batches, dip the fish strips in the batter and deep-fry them for 3–5 minutes, or until crisp. Using a slotted spoon, remove the strips and drain on absorbent kitchen paper.

Meanwhile, make the sauce. Place 3 tablespoons of the orange juice, the vinegar, sherry, soy sauce, sugar, tomato purée and red pepper in a small saucepan. Bring to the boil, lower the heat and simmer for 3 minutes.

Blend the cornflour with the remaining orange juice, stir into the sauce and simmer, stirring, for 1 minute or until thickened. Arrange the fish on a warmed platter or individual plates. Drizzle a little of the sauce over and serve immediately with the remaining sauce.

Cantonese Chicken Wings

Serves 4

3 tbsp hoisin sauce
2 tbsp dark soy sauce
1 tbsp sesame oil
1 garlic clove, peeled and crushed
2.5 cm/1 inch piece fresh root
ginger, peeled and grated
1 tbsp Chinese rice wine or
dry sherry
2 tsp chilli bean sauce
2 tsp red or white wine vinegar
2 tbsp soft light brown sugar
900 g/2 lb large chicken wings
50 g/2 oz cashew nuts, chopped
2 spring onions, trimmed and
finely chopped

Preheat the oven to 220°C/ 425°F/Gas Mark 7, 15 minutes before cooking. Place the hoisin sauce, soy sauce, sesame oil, garlic, ginger, Chinese rice wine or sherry, chilli bean sauce, vinegar and sugar in a small saucepan with 6 tablespoons of water. Bring to the boil, stirring occasionally, then simmer for about 30 seconds. Remove the glaze from the heat.

Place the chicken wings in a roasting tin in a single layer. Pour over the glaze and stir until the wings are coated thoroughly.

Cover the tin loosely with tinfoil, place in the preheated oven and roast for 25 minutes. Remove the tinfoil, baste the wings and cook for a further 5 minutes.

Reduce the oven temperature to 190°C/375°F/Gas Mark 5. Turn the wings over and sprinkle with the chopped cashew nuts and spring onions. Return to the oven and cook for 5 minutes, or until the nuts are lightly browned, the glaze is sticky and the wings are tender. Remove from the oven and leave to stand for 5 minutes before arranging on a warmed platter. Serve immediately with finger bowls and plenty of napkins.

Thai Chicken Wings

Serves 4

4 tbsp clear honey
1 tbsp chilli sauce
1 garlic clove, peeled and crushed
1 tsp freshly grated root ginger
1 lemon grass stalk, outer leaves
discarded and finely chopped
2 tbsp lime zest
3–4 tbsp freshly squeezed
lime juice
1 tbsp light soy sauce
1 tsp ground cumin
1 tsp ground coriander
$1/4$ tsp ground cinnamon
1.4 kg/3 lb chicken wings (about
12 large wings)
6 tbsp mayonnaise
2 tbsp freshly chopped coriander
lemon or lime wedges, to garnish

Preheat the oven to 190°C/ 375°F/Gas Mark 5, 10 minutes before cooking. In a small saucepan, mix together the honey, chilli sauce, garlic, ginger, lemon grass, 1 tablespoon of the lime zest and 2 tablespoons of the lime juice with the soy sauce, cumin, coriander and cinnamon. Heat gently until just starting to bubble, then remove from the heat and leave to cool.

Prepare the chicken wings by folding the tips back under the thickest part of the meat to form a triangle. Arrange in a shallow ovenproof dish. Pour over the honey mixture, turning the wings to ensure that they are all well coated. Cover with clingfilm and leave to marinate in the refrigerator for 4 hours or overnight, turning once or twice.

Mix together the mayonnaise with the remaining lime zest and juice and the coriander. Leave to let the flavours develop while the wings are cooking.

Arrange the wings on a rack set over a tinfoil-lined roasting tin. Roast at the top of the preheated oven for 50–60 minutes, or until the wings are tender and golden, basting once or twice with the remaining marinade and turning once. Remove from the oven. Garnish the wings with lemon or lime wedges and serve immediately with the mayonnaise.

Sticky Braised Spare Ribs

Serves 4

900 g/2 lb meaty pork spare ribs,
cut crossways into
7.5 cm/3 inch pieces
125 ml/4 fl oz apricot nectar or
orange juice
50 ml/2 fl oz dry white wine
3 tbsp black bean sauce
3 tbsp tomato ketchup
2 tbsp clear honey
3–4 spring onions, trimmed
and chopped
2 garlic cloves, peeled
and crushed
grated zest of 1 small orange
salt and freshly ground
black pepper

To garnish:

spring onion tassels
lemon wedges

Put the spare ribs in the wok and add enough cold water to cover. Bring to the boil over a medium-high heat, skimming any scum that rises to the surface. Cover and simmer for 30 minutes, then drain and rinse the ribs.

Rinse and dry the wok and return the ribs to it. In a bowl, blend the apricot nectar or orange juice with the white wine, black bean sauce, tomato ketchup and the honey until smooth.

Stir in the spring onions, garlic cloves and grated orange zest. Stir well until mixed thoroughly.

Pour the mixture over the spare ribs in the wok and stir gently until the ribs are lightly coated. Place over a moderate heat and bring to the boil.

Cover then simmer, stirring occasionally, for 1 hour, or until the ribs are tender and the sauce is thickened and sticky. (If the sauce reduces too quickly or begins to stick, add water 1 tablespoon at a time until the ribs are tender.) Adjust the seasoning to taste, then transfer the ribs to a serving plate and garnish with spring onion tassels and lemon wedges. Serve immediately.

Spring Rolls

Makes 26–30

15 g/¹/₂ oz dried Chinese (shiitake) mushrooms; 50 g/2 oz rice vermicelli; 1–2 tbsp groundnut oil 1 small onion, peeled and finely chopped; 3–4 garlic cloves, peeled and finely chopped; 4 cm/1¹/₂ inch piece fresh root ginger, peeled and chopped; 225 g/8 oz fresh pork mince; 2 spring onions, trimmed and finely chopped; 75 g/3 oz beansprouts; 4 water chestnuts, chopped; 2 tbsp freshly snipped chives; 175 g/6 oz cooked peeled prawns, chopped; 1 tsp oyster sauce; 1 tsp soy sauce; salt and freshly ground black pepper; 4–5 tbsp plain flour 26–30 spring roll wrappers 300 ml/¹/₂ pint vegetable oil for deep frying spring onion tassels, to garnish

Soak the Chinese mushrooms in almost boiling water for 20 minutes. Remove and squeeze out the liquid. Discard any stems, slice and reserve. Soak the rice vermicelli as per the packet instructions.

Heat a large wok and when hot, add the oil. Heat then add the onion, garlic and ginger and stir-fry for 2 minutes. Add the pork, spring onions and Chinese mushrooms and stir-fry for 4 minutes. Stir in the beansprouts, water chestnuts, chives, prawns, oyster and soy sauce. Season to taste with salt and pepper and spoon into a bowl. Drain the noodles well, add to the bowl and toss until well mixed, then leave to cool.

Blend the flour to a smooth paste with 3–4 tablespoons of water. Soften a wrapper in a plate of warm water for 1–2 seconds, then drain. Put 2 tablespoons of the filling near one edge of the wrapper, fold the edge over the filling, then fold in each side and roll up. Seal with a little flour paste and transfer to a baking sheet, seam-side down. Repeat with the remaining wrappers.

Heat the oil in a large wok to 190°C/375°F, or until a cube of bread browns in 30 seconds. Fry the spring rolls a few at a time, until golden. Remove and drain on absorbent kitchen paper. Arrange on a serving plate and garnish with spring onion tassels. Serve immediately.

Vegetable Thai Spring Rolls ⓥ

Serves 4

50 g/2 oz cellophane vermicelli
4 dried shiitake mushrooms
1 tbsp groundnut oil
2 medium carrots, peeled and cut into fine matchsticks
125 g/4 oz mangetout, cut lengthways into fine strips
3 spring onions, trimmed and chopped
125 g/4 oz canned bamboo shoots, cut into fine matchsticks
1 cm/½ inch piece fresh root ginger, peeled and grated
1 tbsp light soy sauce
1 medium egg, separated
salt and freshly ground black pepper
20 spring roll wrappers, each about 12.5 cm/5 inch square
vegetable oil for deep-frying
spring onion tassels, to garnish

Place the vermicelli in a bowl and pour over enough boiling water to cover. Leave to soak for 5 minutes or until softened, then drain. Cut into 7.5 cm/3 inch lengths. Soak the shiitake mushrooms in almost boiling water for 15 minutes, drain, discard the stalks and slice thinly.

Heat a wok or large frying pan, add the groundnut oil and when hot, add the carrots and stir-fry for 1 minute. Add the mangetout and spring onions and stir-fry for 2–3 minutes or until tender. Tip the vegetables into a bowl and leave to cool. Stir the vermicelli and shiitake mushrooms into the cooled vegetables with the bamboo shoots, ginger, soy sauce and egg yolk. Season to taste with salt and pepper and mix thoroughly.

Brush the edges of a spring roll wrapper with a little beaten egg white. Spoon 2 teaspoons of the vegetable filling on to the wrapper, in a 7.5 cm/ 3 inch log shape 2.5 cm/1 inch from one edge. Fold the wrapper edge over the filling, then fold in the right and left sides. Brush the folded edges with more egg white and roll up neatly. Place on an oiled baking sheet, seam-side down and make the rest of the spring rolls.

Heat the oil in a heavy-based saucepan or deep-fat fryer to 180˚C/350˚F. Deep-fry the spring rolls, 6 at a time for 2–3 minutes, or until golden brown and crisp. Drain on absorbent kitchen paper and arrange on a warmed platter. Garnish with spring onion tassels and serve immediately.

Popcorn ❧ Sesame Pecans Ⓥ

Serves 4–6

For the popcorn:

75 ml/ 3 fl oz vegetable oil
75 g/3 oz unpopped popcorn
$\frac{1}{2}$ tsp garlic salt
1 tsp hot chilli powder

For the pecans:

50 g/2 oz granulated sugar
$\frac{1}{2}$ tsp ground cinnamon
$\frac{1}{2}$ tsp ground Chinese five
spice powder
$\frac{1}{4}$ tsp salt
$\frac{1}{4}$ tsp cayenne pepper
175 g/6 oz pecan or walnut halves
sesame seeds for sprinkling

For the popcorn, heat half the oil in a large wok over a medium-high heat. Add 2–3 kernels and cover with a lid. When these kernels pop, add all the popcorn and cover tightly. Cook until the popping stops, shaking from time to time.

When the popping stops, pour the popped corn into a bowl and immediately add the remaining oil to the wok with the garlic salt and chilli powder. Stir-fry for 30 seconds, or until blended and fragrant. Return the popcorn to the wok, stir-fry and toss for a further 30 seconds, or until coated. Pour into the bowl and serve warm or at room temperature.

For the pecans, put the sugar, cinnamon, Chinese five spice powder, salt and cayenne pepper into a large wok and stir in 50 ml/2 fl oz water. Bring to the boil over a high heat, then simmer for 4 minutes, stirring frequently.

Remove from the heat and stir in the pecans or walnuts until well coated. Turn onto a lightly oiled, non-stick baking sheet and sprinkle generously with the sesame seeds.

Working quickly with 2 forks, separate the nuts into individual pieces or bite-sized clusters. Sprinkle with a few more sesame seeds and leave to cool completely. Carefully remove from the baking sheet, breaking into smaller pieces if necessary.

Stir-fried Cheese & Spicy Nuts Ⓥ

Serves 12

For the stir-fried cheese canapés:

6 thick slices white bread
40 g/1 1/2 oz butter, softened
75 g/3 oz mature Cheddar, cheese grated
75 g/3 oz blue cheese such as Stilton or Gorgonzola, crumbled (look for vegetarian varieties of blue cheese if needed)
3 tbsp sunflower oil

For the spicy nuts:

25 g/1 oz unsalted butter
2 tbsp light olive oil
450 g/1 lb mixed unsalted nuts
1 tsp ground paprika
1/2 tsp ground cumin
1/2 tsp fine sea salt
sprigs of fresh coriander, to garnish

For the cheese canapés, cut the crusts off the bread, then gently roll with a rolling pin to flatten slightly. Thinly spread with butter, then sprinkle over the mixed cheeses as evenly as possible.

Roll up each slice tightly, then cut into 4 slices, each about 2.5 cm/ 1 inch long. Heat the oil in a wok or large frying pan and stir-fry the cheese rolls in 2 batches, turning them all the time until golden brown and crisp. Drain on absorbent kitchen paper and serve warm or cold.

For the spicy nuts, melt the butter and oil in a wok, then add the nuts and stir-fry over a low heat for about 5 minutes, stirring all the time, or until they begin to colour.

Sprinkle the paprika and cumin over the nuts and continue stir-frying for a further 1–2 minutes, or until the nuts are golden brown.

Remove from the wok and drain on absorbent kitchen paper. Sprinkle with the salt, garnish with sprigs of fresh coriander and serve hot or cold. If serving cold, store both the cheese canapés and the spicy nuts in airtight containers.

Barbecue Pork Steamed Buns

Serves 12

For the buns:
175–200 g/6–7 oz plain flour
1 tbsp dried yeast
125 ml/4 fl oz milk
2 tbsp sunflower oil
1 tbsp sugar
$^{1}/_{2}$ tsp salt
spring onion tassels, to garnish
fresh green salad leaves,
to serve

For the filling:
2 tbsp vegetable oil
1 small red pepper, deseeded and
finely chopped
2 garlic cloves, peeled and
finely chopped
225 g/8 oz cooked pork,
finely chopped
50 g/2 oz light brown sugar
50 ml/2 fl oz tomato ketchup
1–2 tsp hot chilli powder, or to taste

Put 75 g/3 oz of the flour in a bowl and stir in the yeast. Heat the milk, oil, sugar and salt in a small saucepan until warm, stirring until the sugar has dissolved. Pour into the bowl and, with an electric mixer, beat on a low speed for 30 seconds, scraping down the sides of the bowl, until blended. Beat at high speed for 3 minutes, then, with a wooden spoon, stir in as much of the remaining flour as possible, until a stiff dough forms. Shape into a ball, place in a lightly oiled bowl, cover with clingfilm and leave for 1 hour in a warm place, or until doubled in size.

Heat a wok, add the oil and, when hot, add the red pepper and garlic. Stir-fry for 4–5 minutes. Add the remaining ingredients and bring to the boil, stir-frying for 2–3 minutes until thick and syrupy. Cool and reserve.

Punch down the dough and turn onto a lightly floured surface. Divide into 12 pieces and shape into balls, then cover and leave to rest for 5 minutes. Shape each ball to a 7.5 cm/3 inch circle. Place a heaped tablespoon of filling in the centre of each. Dampen the edges, then bring them up and around the filling, pinching together to seal. Place seam-side down on a small square of nonstick baking parchment. Make the rest. Leave to rise for 10 minutes. Bring a large wok half-filled with water to the boil, place the buns in a lightly oiled Chinese steamer, without touching each other. Cover and steam for 20–25 minutes, then remove and cool slightly. Garnish with spring onion tassels and serve with salad leaves.

Dim Sum Pork Parcels

Makes about 40

125 g/4 oz canned water chestnuts,
drained and finely chopped
125 g/4 oz raw prawns, peeled,
deveined and coarsely chopped
350 g/12 oz fresh pork mince
2 tbsp smoked bacon,
finely chopped
1 tbsp light soy sauce, plus extra,
to serve
1 tsp dark soy sauce
1 tbsp Chinese rice wine
2 tbsp fresh root ginger, peeled and
finely chopped
3 spring onions, trimmed and
finely chopped
2 tsp sesame oil
1 medium egg white, lightly beaten
salt and freshly ground black pepper
2 tsp granulated sugar
40 wonton skins, thawed if frozen
toasted sesame seeds, to garnish
soy sauce, to serve

Place the water chestnuts, prawns, pork mince and bacon in a bowl and mix together. Add the soy sauces, Chinese rice wine, ginger, chopped spring onion, sesame oil and egg white. Season to taste with salt and pepper, sprinkle in the sugar and mix the filling thoroughly.

Place a spoonful of filling in the centre of a wonton skin. Bring the sides up and press around the filling to make a basket shape. Flatten the base of the skin, so the wonton stands solid. The top should be wide open, exposing the filling.

Place the parcels on a heatproof plate, on a wire rack inside a wok or on the base of a muslin-lined bamboo steamer. Place over a wok, half-filled with boiling water, cover, then steam the parcels for about 20 minutes. Do this in two batches. Transfer to a warmed serving plate, sprinkle with toasted sesame seeds, drizzle with soy sauce and serve immediately.

Deep-fried Crab Wontons

Makes 24–30

2 tbsp sesame oil
6–8 water chestnuts, rinsed,
drained and chopped
2 spring onions, peeled and
finely chopped
1 cm/$^1/_2$ inch piece fresh root ginger,
peeled and grated
185 g can white crabmeat, drained
50 ml/2 fl oz soy sauce
2 tbsp rice wine vinegar
$^1/_2$ tsp dried crushed chillies
2 tsp caster sugar
$^1/_2$ tsp hot pepper sauce, or to taste
1 tbsp freshly chopped coriander
or dill
1 large egg yolk
1 packet wonton skins
vegetable oil for deep-frying
lime wedges, to garnish
dipping sauce, to serve

Heat a wok or large frying pan, add 1 tablespoon of the sesame oil and when hot, add the water chestnuts, spring onions and ginger and stir-fry for 1 minute. Remove from the heat and leave to cool slightly.

In a bowl, mix the crabmeat with the soy sauce, rice wine vinegar, crushed chillies, sugar, hot pepper sauce, chopped coriander or dill and the egg yolk. Stir in the cooled stir-fried mixture until well blended.

Lay the wonton skins on a work surface and place 1 teaspoonful of the crab mixture on the centre of each. Brush the edges of each wonton skin with a little water and fold up one corner to the opposite corner to form a triangle. Press to seal. Bring the two corners of the triangle together to meet in the centre, brush one with a little water and overlap them, pressing to seal and form a 'tortellini' shape. Place on a baking sheet and continue with the remaining triangles.

Pour enough oil into a large wok to come 5 cm/2 inches up the sides and place over a high heat. Working in batches of five or six, fry the wontons for 3 minutes, or until crisp and golden, turning once or twice. Carefully remove the wontons with a slotted spoon, drain on absorbent kitchen paper and keep warm. Place on individual warmed serving plates, garnish each dish with a lime wedge and serve immediately with the dipping sauce.

Swedish Cocktail Meatballs

Serves 4–6

50 g/2 oz butter
1 onion, peeled and finely chopped
50 g/2 oz fresh white breadcrumbs
1 medium egg, beaten
125 ml/4 fl oz double cream
salt and freshly ground
black pepper
350 g/12 oz fresh lean
beef mince
125 g/4 oz fresh pork mince
3–4 tbsp freshly chopped dill
1/2 tsp ground allspice
1 tbsp vegetable oil
125 ml/4 fl oz beef stock
cream cheese and chive or
cranberry sauce, to serve

Heat half the butter in a large wok, add the onion and cook, stirring frequently, for 4–6 minutes, or until softened and beginning to colour. Transfer to a bowl and leave to cool. Wipe out the wok with absorbent kitchen paper. Add the breadcrumbs and beaten egg with 1–2 tablespoons of cream to the bowl. Season to taste with salt and pepper and stir until well blended. Using your fingertips crumble the beef and pork mince into the bowl. Add half the dill, the allspice and, using your hands, mix together until well blended. With dampened hands, shape the mixture into 2.5 cm/1 inch balls.

Melt the remaining butter in the wok and add the vegetable oil, swirling it to coat the side of the wok. Working in batches, add about one quarter to one third of the meatballs in a single layer and cook for 5 minutes, swirling and turning until golden and cooked. Transfer to a plate and continue with the remaining meatballs.

Pour off the fat in the wok. Add the beef stock and bring to the boil, then boil until reduced by half, stirring and scraping up any browned bits from the bottom. Add the remaining cream and continue to simmer until slightly thickened and reduced. Stir in the remaining dill and season if necessary. Add the meatballs and simmer for 2–3 minutes, or until heated right through. Serve with cocktail sticks, with the sauce in a separate bowl for dipping.

Thai Marinated Prawns

Serves 4

700 g/1$\frac{1}{2}$ lb large raw prawns,
peeled with tails left on
2 large eggs
salt
50 g/2 oz cornflour
vegetable oil for deep-frying
lime wedges, to garnish

For the marinade:

2 lemon grass stalks, outer leaves
discarded and bruised
2 garlic cloves, peeled and
finely chopped
2 shallots, peeled and
finely chopped
1 red chilli, deseeded and chopped
grated zest and juice of 1 small lime
400 ml/14 fl oz coconut milk

Mix all the marinade ingredients together in a bowl, pressing on the solid ingredients to release their flavours. Season to taste with salt and reserve.

Using a sharp knife, remove the black vein along the back of the prawns and pat dry with absorbent kitchen paper. Add the prawns to the marinade and stir gently until coated evenly. Leave in the marinade for at least 1 hour, stirring occasionally.

Beat the eggs in a deep bowl with a little salt. Place the cornflour in a shallow bowl. Using a slotted spoon or spatula, transfer the prawns from the marinade to the cornflour. Stir gently until the prawns are coated on all sides and shake off any excess.

Holding each prawn by its tail, dip it into the beaten egg, then into the cornflour again, shaking off any excess.

Pour enough oil into a large wok to come 5 cm/2 inches up the sides and place over a high heat. Working in batches of five or six, deep-fry the prawns for 2 minutes, or until pink and crisp, turning once. Using a slotted spoon, remove and drain on absorbent kitchen paper. Keep warm. Arrange on a warmed serving plate and garnish with lime wedges. Serve immediately.

Tempura

Serves 4

For the batter:

200 g/7 oz plain flour
pinch bicarbonate of soda
1 medium egg yolk

For the prawns & vegetables:

8–12 raw king size prawns
1 carrot, peeled
125 g/4 oz button mushrooms, wiped
1 green pepper, deseeded
1 small aubergine, trimmed
1 onion, peeled
125 g/4 oz French beans
125 ml/4 fl oz sesame oil
300 ml/$^1/_2$ pint vegetable oil for deep frying

To serve:

soy sauce
chilli dipping sauce

Sift the flour and bicarbonate of soda into a mixing bowl. Blend 450 ml/$^3/_4$ pint water and the egg yolk together, then gradually whisk into the flour mixture until a smooth batter is formed.

Peel the prawns, leaving the tails intact, de-vein, then rinse lightly and pat dry with absorbent kitchen paper and reserve. Slice the carrot thinly then, using small pastry cutters, cut out fancy shapes. Cut the mushrooms in half, if large, and cut the pepper into chunks. Slice the aubergine, then cut into chunks, together with the onion, and finally trim the French beans.

Pour the sesame oil and the vegetable oil into a large wok and heat to 180°C/350°F, or until a small spoonful of the batter dropped into the oil sizzles and cooks on impact.

Dip the prawns and vegetables into the reserved batter (no more than eight pieces at a time) and stir until lightly coated. Cook for 3 minutes, turning occasionally during cooking, or until evenly golden. Using a slotted spoon, transfer the prawns and vegetables onto absorbent kitchen paper and drain well. Keep warm. Repeat with the remaining ingredients. Serve immediately with soy sauce and chilli dipping sauce.

Thai Rice Cakes with Mango Salsa Ⓥ

Serves 4

225 g/8 oz Thai fragrant rice
400 g can coconut milk
1 lemon grass stalk, bruised
2 kaffir lime leaves, shredded
1 tbsp vegetable oil, plus extra for
deep frying
1 garlic clove, peeled and
finely chopped
1 tsp freshly grated root ginger
1 red pepper, deseeded and
finely chopped
2 red chillies, deseeded and
finely chopped
1 medium egg, beaten
25 g/1 oz dried breadcrumbs

For the mango salsa:

1 large mango, peeled, stoned and
finely chopped
1 small red onion, peeled and
finely chopped
2 tbsp each freshly chopped
coriander and basil
juice of 1 lime

Wash the rice in several changes of water until the water stays relatively clear. Drain, place in a saucepan with a tight-fitting lid and add the coconut milk, lemon grass and lime leaves. Bring to the boil, cover and cook over the lowest possible heat for 10 minutes. Turn off the heat and leave to stand for 10 minutes, without lifting the lid.

Heat the wok, then add 1 tablespoon of oil and when hot, add the garlic, ginger, red pepper and half the chilli. Stir-fry for 1–2 minutes until just softened then place in a large bowl.

When the rice is cooked, turn into the mixing bowl and add the egg. Season to taste with salt and pepper and mix together well. Put the breadcrumbs into a shallow dish. Form the rice mixture into eight cakes and coat them in the breadcrumbs. Chill the cakes in the refrigerator for 30 minutes.

Meanwhile, make the mango salsa. In a bowl, mix together the mango, red onion, coriander, basil, lime juice and remaining red chilli and reserve.

Fill a clean wok about one-third full of vegetable oil. Heat to 190°C/375°F, or until a cube of bread browns in 30 seconds. Cook the rice cakes, one or two at a time, for 2–3 minutes until golden and crisp. Drain on absorbent kitchen paper. Serve with the mango salsa.

Thai Stuffed Eggs (V)

Makes 8

4 large eggs
salt and freshly ground
black pepper
225 g/8 oz baby spinach
2 garlic cloves, peeled and crushed
1 tbsp spring onions, trimmed and
finely chopped
1 tbsp sesame seeds
75 g/3 oz plain flour
1 tbsp light olive oil
300 ml/^{1}/$_2$ pint vegetable
oil for frying

To garnish:

sliced red chilli
snipped fresh chives

Bring a small saucepan of water to the boil, add the eggs, bring back to the boil and cook for 6–7 minutes. Plunge into cold water, then shell and cut in half lengthways. Using a teaspoon, remove the yolks and place in a bowl. Reserve the whites.

Place 1 teaspoon of water and ^{1}/$_2$ teaspoon of salt in a saucepan, add the spinach and cook until tender and wilted. Drain, squeeze out the excess moisture and chop. Mix with the egg yolk, then stir in the garlic, spring onions and sesame seeds. Season to taste with salt and pepper. Fill the egg shells with the mixture, smoothing into a mound.

Place the flour in a bowl with the olive oil, a large pinch salt and 125 ml/4 fl oz warm water. Beat together to make a completely smooth batter.

Heat a wok, add the vegetable oil and heat to 180°C/350°F. Dip the stuffed eggs in the batter, allowing any excess batter to drip back into the bowl, and deep-fry in batches for 3–4 minutes or until golden brown. Place the eggs in the wok filled side down first, then turn over to finish cooking. Remove from the wok with a slotted spoon and drain on absorbent kitchen paper. Serve hot or cold garnished with snipped chives and chilli rings.

Onion Bhajis Ⓥ

Serves 4–6

2 large onions, peeled
225 g/8 oz chickpea flour
small piece fresh root ginger,
peeled and grated
$^1/_2$–1 small chilli, deseeded and
finely chopped
$^1/_2$ tsp turmeric
$^1/_2$ tsp ground coriander
4 tbsp freshly chopped coriander
freshly milled salt, to taste
120–150 ml/4–5 fl oz water
vegetable oil, for deep-frying

Finely slice the onions and place in a mixing bowl with the flour, spices and coriander. Add salt to taste.

Slowly stir in the water and mix to form a thick consistency. Form into loose balls.

Heat the oil in deep-fryer to a temperature of 180°C/350°F. Drop the bhajis, about two or three at a time, into the hot oil and deep-fry for 2–3 minutes, or until golden brown and crisp. Remove with a slotted spoon and drain on absorbent kitchen paper. Serve.

Vegetable Samosas Ⓥ

Serves 4–6

150 g/5 oz potatoes, peeled
2–3 tbsp vegetable oil, plus extra
for deep-frying
1 tsp mustard seeds
1 onion, peeled and chopped
1 tsp ground coriander
$1/2$–1 tsp garam masala
$1/2$ tsp turmeric
1–2 red chillies, deseeded
and chopped
2 tbsp water
1 large carrot, peeled and grated
75 g/3 oz frozen peas
75 g/3 oz French beans, trimmed
and chopped
250 g/9 oz filo pastry

Cut the potato into small dice and leave in a bowl of cold water until required. Drain thoroughly and shake dry when ready to use.

Heat 2 tablespoons of the oil in a frying pan, add the mustard seeds and stir-fry for 1 minute, or until they pop. Add the onion and continue to fry for 5–8 minutes, or until softened. Add the remaining oil, if necessary.

Add the spices, chilli and water and cook for a further 3 minutes, then add the potatoes, carrot, peas and beans. Stir, then cover and cook for 10–15 minutes, or until the vegetables are just cooked. Allow to cool.

Cut the pastry into 7.5 cm/3 inch strips. Brush a strip lightly with water and place a second strip on top. Place 1 tablespoon of the filling at one end of the strip then fold the pastry over to form a triangle. Brush the pastry lightly with water. Continue folding the pastry forming triangles to the end of the strip. Repeat with the remaining pastry and filling.

Heat the oil in a deep-fryer to a temperature of 180°C/350°F and deep-fry the samosas, in batches of about two or three at a time, for 2–3 minutes, or until golden. Remove with a slotted spoon and drain on absorbent kitchen paper. Serve hot or cold.

Sweet Mango Chutney Ⓥ

Serves 4–6

4 ripe mangos, about 900 g/2 lb
in weight
1–2 red chillies, deseeded
and chopped
5 cm/2 inch piece fresh root
ginger, peeled and grated
grated rind and juice of 3 lemons,
preferably unwaxed (organic)
600 ml/1 pint water
450 g/1 lb light muscovado sugar
175 g/6 oz golden sultanas
2–3 tbsp balsamic vinegar

Peel, stone and finely chop the mangos and place in a preserving pan together with the chillies and grated ginger.

Add the lemon rind and juice and stir in the water. Bring to the boil, then reduce the heat and simmer for 35–40 minutes, or until the mangos are really soft.

Add the sugar and sultanas to the pan and heat gently until the sugar has dissolved. Bring to the boil and continue to boil for 10 minutes, or until a thick consistency is reached. Stir in the balsamic vinegar and cook for a further 5 minutes. Cool slightly then put in clean sterilised jars and seal when cold.

Meat *and*

Poultry

When it comes to more substantial street eats, meat and poultry, combined with the right spices and seasonings, can be sensational. The intense savoury flavour of Jamaican Jerk Pork will transport you to sunny Caribbean beaches, whilst Pad Thai is a South-East Asian street food classic not to be missed. From Vietnamese-style Aromatic Beef to Spicy Chicken Skewers with Mango Tabbouleh, this is home-made street food at its best.

Chinese Chicken Soup

Serves 4

225 g/8 oz cooked chicken
1 tsp vegetable oil
6 spring onions, trimmed
and diagonally sliced
1 red chilli, deseeded
and finely chopped
1 garlic clove, peeled
and crushed
2.5 cm/1 inch piece
root ginger, peeled
and finely grated
1 litre/1^3/$_4$ pint chicken stock
150 g/5 oz medium
egg noodles
1 carrot, peeled and cut
into matchsticks
125 g/4 oz beansprouts
2 tbsp soy sauce
1 tbsp fish sauce
fresh coriander leaves,
to garnish

Remove any skin from the chicken. Place on a chopping board and use two forks to tear the chicken into fine shreds.

Heat the oil in a large saucepan and fry the spring onions and chilli for 1 minute. Add the garlic and ginger and cook for another minute. Stir in the chicken stock and gradually bring the mixture to the boil.

Break up the noodles a little and add to the boiling stock with the carrot. Stir to mix, then reduce the heat to a simmer and cook for 3–4 minutes.

Add the shredded chicken, beansprouts, soy sauce and fish sauce and stir. Cook for a further 2–3 minutes until piping hot. Ladle the soup into bowls and sprinkle with the coriander leaves. Serve immediately.

Wonton Noodle Soup

Serves 4

4 shiitake mushrooms, wiped
125 g/4 oz raw prawns, peeled and
finely chopped
125 g/4 oz pork mince
4 water chestnuts, finely chopped
4 spring onions, trimmed and
finely sliced
1 medium egg white
salt and freshly ground black pepper
1¹/₂ tsp cornflour
1 packet fresh wonton wrappers
1.1 litres/2 pints chicken stock
2 cm/³/₄ inch piece root ginger,
peeled and sliced
75 g/3 oz thin egg noodles
125 g/4 oz pak choi, shredded

Place the mushrooms in a bowl, cover with warm water and leave to soak for 1 hour. Drain, remove and discard the stalks and finely chop the mushrooms. Return to the bowl with the prawns, pork, water chestnuts, 2 of the spring onions and egg white. Season to taste with salt and pepper. Mix well.

Mix the cornflour with 1 tablespoon of cold water to make a paste. Place a wonton wrapper on a board and brush the edges with the paste. Drop a little less than 1 teaspoon of the pork mixture in the centre then fold in half to make a triangle, pressing the edges together. Bring the two outer corners together, fixing together with a little more paste. Continue until all the pork mixture is used up; you should have 16–20 wontons.

Pour the stock into a large wide saucepan, add the ginger slices and bring to the boil. Add the wontons and simmer for about 5 minutes. Add the noodles and cook for 1 minute. Stir in the pak choi and cook for a further 2 minutes, or until the noodles and pak choi are tender and the wontons have floated to the surface and are cooked through.

Ladle the soup into warmed bowls, discarding the ginger. Sprinkle with the remaining sliced spring onion and serve immediately.

Jamaican Jerk Pork

Serves 4

175 g/6 oz dried red kidney beans,
soaked overnight
2 onions, peeled and chopped
2 garlic cloves, peeled and crushed
4 tbsp lime juice
2 tbsp each dark molasses, soy sauce
and chopped fresh root ginger
2 jalapeño chillies, deseeded
and chopped
1/2 tsp ground cinnamon
1/4 tsp each ground allspice,
ground nutmeg
4 pork loin chops, on the bone

For the rice:
1 tbsp vegetable oil
1 onion, peeled and finely chopped
1 celery stalk, trimmed and finely sliced
3 garlic cloves, peeled and crushed
2 bay leaves
225 g/8 oz long-grain white rice
475 ml/18 fl oz chicken or ham stock
fresh flat-leaf parsley sprigs, to garnish

To make the jerk pork marinade, purée the onions, garlic, lime juice, molasses, soy sauce, ginger, chillies, cinnamon, allspice and nutmeg together in a food processor until smooth. Put the pork chops into a plastic or non-reactive dish and pour over the marinade, turning the chops to coat. Marinate in the refrigerator for at least 1 hour or overnight.

Drain the beans and place in a large saucepan with about 2 litres/ 3 1/2 pints cold water. Bring to the boil and boil rapidly for 10 minutes. Reduce the heat, cover and simmer gently, for 1 hour until tender, adding more water, if necessary. When cooked, drain well and mash roughly.

Heat the oil for the rice in a saucepan with a tight-fitting lid and add the onion, celery and garlic. Cook gently for 5 minutes until softened. Add the bay leaves, rice and stock and stir. Bring to the boil, cover and cook very gently for 10 minutes. Add the beans and stir well again. Cook for a further 5 minutes, then remove from the heat.

Heat a griddle pan until almost smoking. Remove the pork chops from the marinade, scraping off any surplus and add to the hot pan. Cook for 5–8 minutes on each side, or until cooked. Garnish with the parsley and serve immediately with the rice.

Caribbean Chicken & Coconut Soup

Serves 4

6–8 spring onions
2 garlic cloves
1 red chilli
175 g/6 oz cooked chicken,
shredded or diced
2 tbsp vegetable oil
1 tsp ground turmeric
300 ml/^{1}/$_2$ pint coconut milk
900 ml/1^1/$_2$ pints chicken stock
50 g/2 oz small soup pasta or
spaghetti, broken into small pieces
^{1}/$_2$ lemon, sliced
salt and freshly ground
black pepper
1–2 tbsp freshly chopped coriander
sprigs of fresh coriander, to garnish

Trim the spring onions and thinly slice; peel the garlic and finely chop. Cut off the top from the chilli, slit down the side and remove seeds and membrane, then finely chop and reserve.

Remove and discard any skin or bones from the cooked chicken and shred using two forks and reserve.

Heat a large wok, add the oil and when hot add the spring onions, garlic and chilli and stir-fry for 2 minutes, or until the onion has softened. Stir in the turmeric and cook for 1 minute.

Blend the coconut milk with the chicken stock until smooth, then pour into the wok. Add the pasta or spaghetti with the lemon slices and bring to the boil. Simmer, half-covered, for 10–12 minutes, or until the pasta is tender; stir occasionally.

Remove the lemon slices from the wok and add the chicken. Season to taste with salt and pepper and simmer for 2–3 minutes, or until the chicken is heated through thoroughly. Stir in the chopped coriander and ladle into heated bowls. Garnish with sprigs of fresh coriander and serve immediately.

Caribbean Pork

Serves 4

450 g/1 lb pork fillet
2.5 cm/1 inch piece fresh root
ginger, peeled and grated
$^{1}/_{2}$ tsp crushed dried chillies
2 garlic cloves, peeled and crushed
2 tbsp freshly chopped parsley
150 ml/$^{1}/_{4}$ pint orange juice
2 tbsp dark soy sauce
2 tbsp groundnut oil
1 large onion, peeled and sliced
into wedges
1 large courgette (about
225 g/8 oz), trimmed and
cut into strips
1 orange pepper, deseeded and
cut into strips
1 ripe but firm mango, peeled
and pitted
freshly cooked rice to serve

Cut the pork fillet into thin strips and place in a shallow dish. Sprinkle with the ginger, chillies, garlic and 1 tablespoon of the parsley. Blend together the orange juice, soy sauce and 1 tablespoon of the oil, then pour over the pork. Cover and chill in the refrigerator for 30 minutes, stirring occasionally. Remove the pork strips with a slotted spoon and reserve the marinade.

Heat the wok, pour in the remaining oil and stir-fry the pork for 3–4 minutes. Add the onion rings and the courgette and pepper strips and cook for 2 minutes. Add the reserved marinade to the wok and stir-fry for a further 2 minutes.

Remove the stone from the mango, cut the flesh into strips, then stir it into the pork mixture. Continue to stir-fry until everything is piping hot. Garnish with the remaining parsley and serve immediately with plenty of freshly cooked rice.

New Orleans Jambalaya

Serves 6–8

For the seasoning mix:

2 dried bay leaves; 1 tsp salt
2 tsp cayenne pepper, or to taste
2 tsp dried oregano; 1 tsp each ground
white and black pepper, or to taste

For the jambalaya:

3 tbsp vegetable oil; 125 g/4 oz ham
225 g/8 oz smoked pork sausage, cut
into chunks; 2 large onions, peeled
and chopped; 4 celery stalks,
trimmed and chopped; 2 green
peppers, deseeded and chopped
2 garlic cloves, peeled and
finely chopped
350 g/12 oz raw chicken, diced
400 g can chopped tomatoes
600 ml/1 pint fish stock
400 g/14 oz long-grain white rice
4 spring onions, trimmed and
coarsely chopped
275 g/10 oz raw prawns, peeled
250 g/9 oz white crab meat

Mix all the seasoning ingredients together in a small bowl and reserve.

Heat 2 tablespoons of the oil in a large flameproof casserole over a medium heat. Add the ham and sausage and cook, stirring often, for 7–8 minutes until golden. Remove from the pan and reserve.

Add the remaining onions, celery and peppers to the casserole and cook for about 4 minutes, or until softened, stirring occasionally. Stir in the garlic, then using a slotted spoon, transfer all the vegetables to a plate and reserve with the sausage.

Add the chicken pieces to the casserole and cook for about 4 minutes, or until beginning to colour, turning once. Stir in the seasoning mix and turn the pieces to coat well. Return the sausage and vegetables to the casserole and stir well. Add the chopped tomatoes, with their juice, and the stock and bring to the boil.

Stir in the rice and reduce the heat to low. Cover and simmer for 12 minutes. Uncover, stir in the spring onions and prawns and cook, covered, for a further 4 minutes. Add the crab and gently stir in. Cook for 2–3 minutes, or until the rice is tender. Remove from the heat, cover and leave to stand for 5 minutes before serving.

Vietnamese Beef & Noodle Soup

Serves 4–6

For the beef stock:

900 g/2 lb meaty beef bones
1 large onion, peeled and quartered
2 carrots, peeled and cut into chunks
2 celery stalks, trimmed and sliced
1 leek, washed and sliced
into chunks
2 garlic cloves, unpeeled and
lightly crushed
3 whole star anise
1 tsp black peppercorns

For the soup:

175 g/6 oz dried rice stick noodles
4–6 spring onions, trimmed and
diagonally sliced
1 red chilli, deseeded and
diagonally sliced
1 small bunch fresh coriander
1 small bunch fresh mint
350 g/12 oz fillet steak, very
thinly sliced
salt and freshly ground black pepper

Place all the ingredients for the beef stock into a large stock pot or saucepan and cover with cold water. Bring to the boil and skim off any scum that rises to the surface. Reduce the heat and simmer gently, partially covered, for 2–3 hours, skimming occasionally.

Strain into a large bowl and leave to cool, then skim off the fat. Chill in the refrigerator and when cold remove any fat from the surface. Pour 1.7 litres/3 pints of the stock into a large wok and reserve.

Cover the noodles with warm water and leave for 3 minutes, or until just softened. Drain, then cut into 10 cm/4 inch lengths.

Arrange the spring onions and chilli on a serving platter or large plate. Strip the leaves from the coriander and mint and arrange them in piles on the plate.

Bring the stock in the wok to the boil over a high heat. Add the noodles and simmer for about 2 minutes, or until tender. Add the beef strips and simmer for about 1 minute. Season to taste with salt and pepper.

Ladle the soup with the noodles and beef strips into individual soup bowls and serve immediately with the plate of condiments handed around separately.

Vietnamese-style Aromatic Beef

Serves 4–6

550 g/1¼ lb stewing steak
2 tbsp vegetable oil
5 cardamom pods, cracked
1 cinnamon stick, bruised
3 whole star anise
2 lemon grass stalks, outer leaves
discarded and bruised
1 small green chilli, deseeded
and chopped
1–2 tbsp medium hot curry paste
2 red onions, peeled and cut
into wedges
2 garlic cloves, peeled and sliced
450 ml/¾ pint beef stock
150 ml/¼ pint coconut milk
1 tbsp soy sauce
225 g/8 oz carrots, peeled
and sliced
175 g/6 oz sugar snap peas

Trim the meat, cut into bite-sized chunks and reserve. Heat the
oil in a large heavy-based frying pan, add the cardamom pods,
cinnamon stick, star anise and lemon grass and gently fry for
2 minutes. Add the chilli and continue to fry for a further 2 minutes.

Add the meat to the pan and stir-fry for 5 minutes, or until the
meat is sealed.

Add the curry paste and the onions and garlic and fry for a further
5 minutes before stirring in the beef stock and coconut milk.

Bring to the boil, then reduce the heat, cover and simmer for
1½ hours, stirring occasionally. Add the soy sauce and carrots
and continue to cook for a further 30 minutes. Add the sugar snap
peas and cook for 10 minutes, or until the meat and vegetables are
tender. Remove the cinnamon stick and whole anise and serve.

Laksa Malayan Rice Noodle Soup

Serves 4–6

1.1 kg/2$^1/_2$ lb free-range chicken
1 tsp black peppercorns
1 tbsp vegetable oil
1 large onion, peeled and thinly sliced
2 garlic cloves, peeled and
finely chopped
2.5 cm/1 inch piece fresh root ginger,
peeled and thinly sliced
1 tsp ground coriander
2 red chillies, deseeded and
diagonally sliced
1–2 tsp hot curry paste
400 ml/14 fl oz coconut milk
450 g/1 lb large raw prawns, peeled
and deveined
$^1/_2$ small head of Chinese leaves,
thinly shredded
1 tsp sugar; 2 spring onions, trimmed
and thinly sliced
125 g/4 oz beansprouts
250 g/9 oz rice noodles or rice sticks,
soaked as per packet instructions
fresh mint leaves, to garnish

Put the chicken in a large saucepan with the peppercorns and cover with cold water. Bring to the boil, skimming off any scum that rises to the surface. Simmer, partially covered, for about 1 hour. Remove the chicken and cool. Skim any fat from the stock and strain through a muslin-lined sieve and reserve. Remove the meat from the carcass, shred and reserve.

Heat a large wok, add the oil and when hot, add the onions and stir-fry for 2 minutes, or until they begin to colour. Stir in the garlic, ginger, coriander, chillies and curry paste and stir-fry for a further 2 minutes.

Carefully pour in the reserved stock (you need at least 1.1 litres/ 2 pints) and simmer gently, partially covered, for 10 minutes, or until slightly reduced.

Add the coconut milk, prawns, Chinese leaves, sugar, spring onions and beansprouts and simmer for 3 minutes, stirring occasionally. Add the reserved shredded chicken, and cook for a further 2 minutes.

Drain the noodles and divide between 4–6 soup bowls. Ladle the hot stock and vegetables over the noodles, making sure each serving has some prawns and chicken. Garnish each bowl with fresh mint leaves and serve immediately.

Teriyaki Turkey with Vegetables

Serves 4

1 red chilli
1 garlic clove, peeled and crushed
2.5 cm/1 inch piece root ginger, peeled and grated
3 tbsp dark soy sauce
1 tsp sunflower oil
350 g/12 oz skinless, boneless turkey breast
1 tbsp sesame oil
1 tbsp sesame seeds
2 carrots, peeled and cut into matchstick strips
1 leek, trimmed and shredded
125 g/4 oz broccoli, cut into tiny florets
1 tsp cornflour
3 tbsp dry sherry
125 g/4 oz mangetout, cut into thin strips

To serve:
freshly cooked egg noodles
sprinkling of sesame seeds

Halve, deseed and thinly slice the chilli. Put into a small bowl with the garlic, ginger, soy sauce and sunflower oil.

Cut the turkey into thin strips. Add to the mixture and mix until well coated. Cover with clingfilm and marinate in the refrigerator for at least 30 minutes.

Heat a wok or large frying pan. Add 2 teaspoons of the sesame oil. When hot, remove the turkey from the marinade. Stir-fry for 2–3 minutes until browned and cooked. Remove from the pan and reserve.

Heat the remaining 1 teaspoon of oil in the wok. Add the sesame seeds and stir-fry for a few seconds until they start to change colour.

Add the carrots, leek and broccoli and continue stir-frying for 2–3 minutes.

Blend the cornflour with 1 tablespoon of cold water to make a smooth paste. Stir in the sherry and marinade. Add to the wok with the mangetout and cook for 1 minute, stirring all the time until thickened.

Return the turkey to the pan and continue cooking for 1–2 minutes or until the turkey is hot, the vegetables are tender and the sauce is bubbling. Serve the turkey and vegetables immediately with the egg noodles. Sprinkle with the sesame seeds.

Pad Thai

Serves 4

225 g/8 oz flat rice noodles
2 tbsp vegetable oil
225 g/8 oz boneless chicken breast,
skinned and thinly sliced
4 shallots, peeled and thinly sliced
2 garlic cloves, peeled and finely
chopped; 4 spring onions, trimmed
and diagonally cut into 5 cm/2 inch
pieces; 350 g/12 oz fresh white
crab meat or tiny prawns
75 g/3 oz fresh bean sprouts, rinsed
and drained; 2 tbsp preserved or
fresh radish, chopped
2–3 tbsp roasted peanuts, chopped
(optional)

For the sauce:

3 tbsp Thai fish sauce (nam pla)
2–3 tbsp rice vinegar or cider vinegar
1 tbsp chilli bean or oyster sauce
1 tbsp toasted sesame oil
1 tbsp light brown sugar
1 red chilli, deseeded and thinly sliced

To make the sauce, whisk all the sauce ingredients in a bowl and reserve. Put the rice noodles in a large bowl and pour over enough hot water to cover. Leave to stand for about 15 minutes until softened. Drain and rinse, then drain again.

Heat the oil in a wok over a high heat until hot, but not smoking. Add the chicken strips and stir-fry constantly until they begin to colour. Using a slotted spoon, transfer to a plate. Reduce the heat to medium-high.

Add the shallots, garlic and spring onions and stir-fry for 1 minute. Stir in the rice noodles, then the reserved sauce; mix well.

Add the reserved chicken strips, with the crab meat or prawns, bean sprouts and radish and stir well. Cook for about 5 minutes, stirring frequently, until heated through. If the noodles begin to stick, add a little water.

Turn into a large shallow serving dish and sprinkle with the chopped peanuts, if desired. Serve immediately.

Red Chicken Curry

Serves 4

225 ml/8 fl oz coconut cream
2 tbsp vegetable oil
2 garlic cloves, peeled and
finely chopped
2 tbsp Thai red curry paste
2 tbsp Thai fish sauce
2 tsp granulated or palm sugar
350 g/12 oz boneless, skinless
chicken breast, finely sliced
450 ml/³⁄₄ pint chicken stock
2 lime leaves, shredded
chopped red chilli, to garnish
freshly boiled rice or steamed Thai
fragrant rice, to serve

Pour the coconut cream into a small saucepan and heat gently. Meanwhile, heat a wok or large frying pan and add the oil. When the oil is very hot, swirl the oil around the wok until the wok is lightly coated, then add the garlic and stir-fry for about 10–20 seconds, or until the garlic begins to brown. Add the curry paste and stir-fry for a few more seconds, then pour in the warmed coconut cream.

Cook the coconut cream mixture for 5 minutes, or until the cream has curdled and thickened. Stir in the fish sauce and sugar. Add the finely sliced chicken breast and cook for 3–4 minutes, or until the chicken has turned white.

Pour the stock into the wok, bring to the boil, then simmer for 1–2 minutes, or until the chicken is cooked through. Stir in the shredded lime leaves. Turn into a warmed serving dish, garnish with chopped red chilli and serve immediately with rice.

Green Chicken Curry

Serves 4

1 onion, peeled and chopped
3 lemon grass stalks, outer leaves
discarded and finely sliced
2 garlic cloves, peeled and
finely chopped
1 tbsp freshly grated root ginger
3 green chillies
zest and juice of 1 lime
2 tbsp groundnut oil
2 tbsp Thai fish sauce
6 tbsp freshly chopped coriander
6 tbsp freshly chopped basil
450 g/1 lb skinless, boneless
chicken breasts, cut into strips
125 g /4 oz fine green
beans, trimmed
400 ml can coconut milk
fresh basil leaves, to garnish
freshly cooked rice, to serve

Place the onion, lemon grass, garlic, ginger, chillies, lime zest and juice, 1 tablespoon of groundnut oil, the fish sauce, coriander and basil in a food processor. Blend to a form a smooth paste, which should be of a spoonable consistency. If the sauce looks thick, add a little water. Remove and reserve.

Heat the wok, add the remaining 1 tablespoon of oil and when hot add the chicken. Stir-fry for 2–3 minutes, until the chicken starts to colour, then add the green beans and stir-fry for a further minute. Remove the chicken and beans from the wok and reserve. Wipe the wok clean with absorbent kitchen paper.

Spoon the reserved green paste into the wok and heat for 1 minute. Add the coconut milk and whisk to blend. Return the chicken and beans to the wok and bring to the boil. Simmer for 5–7 minutes, or until the chicken is cooked. Sprinkle with basil leaves and serve immediately with freshly cooked rice.

Goan-style Beef Curry

Serves 4–6

2 onions, peeled and chopped
2–3 garlic cloves, peeled
and chopped
5 cm/2 inch piece fresh root ginger,
peeled and grated
1 tsp chilli powder
1 tsp turmeric
1 tsp ground coriander
1 tsp ground cumin
freshly milled salt
450 g/1 lb braising steak, trimmed
2 tbsp vegetable oil
2 green chillies, deseeded and cut
in half lengthways
2 red chillies, deseeded and cut in
half lengthways
450 ml/³/₄ pint beef stock

Place the onions, garlic, ginger and spices in a food processor and blend to a paste.

Spread half the paste half over the steak, then sprinkle lightly with salt. Leave to marinate in the refrigerator for at least 15 minutes.

Cut the beef into small strips. Heat 1 tablespoon of the oil in a heavy-based saucepan, add the beef and fry on all sides for 5 minutes, or until sealed. Remove from the pan and reserve.

Add the remaining oil to the pan, then add the halved chillies and fry for 2 minutes. Remove and reserve. Stir the remaining paste into the oil left in the pan and cook for a further 3 minutes. Return the beef to the pan with the beef stock and bring to the boil.

Reduce the heat, cover and simmer for 30–40 minutes, or until tender. Garnish with the halved chillies and serve.

Chicken ❧ Pepper Curried Rice

Serves 4

350 g/12 oz long-grain rice
salt
1 large egg white
1 tbsp cornflour
300 g/11 oz skinless chicken breast
fillets, cut into chunks
3 tbsp groundnut oil
1 red pepper, deseeded and
roughly chopped
1 tbsp curry powder or paste
125 ml/4 fl oz chicken stock
1 tsp granulated sugar
1 tbsp Chinese rice wine or
dry sherry
1 tbsp light soy sauce
sprigs of fresh coriander, to garnish

Wash the rice in several changes of water until the water remains relatively clear. Drain well. Put into a saucepan and cover with fresh water. Add a little salt and bring to the boil. Cook for 7–8 minutes until tender. Drain and refresh under cold running water, then drain again and reserve.

Lightly whisk the egg white with 1 teaspoon of salt and 2 teaspoons of cornflour until smooth. Add the chicken and mix together well. Cover and chill in the refrigerator for 20 minutes.

Heat the oil in a wok until moderately hot. Add the chicken mixture to the wok and stir-fry for 2–3 minutes until all the chicken has turned white. Using a slotted spoon, lift the cubes of chicken from the wok, then drain on absorbent kitchen paper.

Add the red peppers to the wok and stir-fry for 1 minute over a high heat. Add the curry powder or paste and cook for a further 30 seconds, then add the chicken stock, sugar, Chinese rice wine and soy sauce.

Mix the remaining cornflour with 1 teaspoon of cold water and add to the wok, stirring. Bring to the boil and simmer gently for 1 minute. Return the chicken to the wok, then simmer for a further 1 minute before adding the rice. Stir over a medium heat for another 2 minutes until heated through. Garnish with the sprigs of coriander and serve.

Thai Chicken Fried Rice

Serves 4

175 g/6 oz boneless, chicken breast
2 tbsp vegetable oil
2 garlic cloves, peeled and
finely chopped
2 tsp medium curry paste
450 g/1 lb cold cooked rice
1 tbsp light soy sauce
2 tbsp Thai fish sauce
large pinch granulated sugar
freshly ground black pepper

To garnish:

2 spring onions, trimmed and
shredded lengthways
$^1/_2$ small onion, peeled and very
finely sliced

Using a sharp knife, trim the chicken, discarding any sinew or fat and cut into small cubes. Reserve.

Heat a wok or large frying pan, add the oil and when hot, add the garlic and cook for 10–20 seconds or until just golden. Add the curry paste and stir-fry for a few seconds. Add the chicken and stir-fry for 3–4 minutes, or until tender and the chicken has turned white.

Stir the cold cooked rice into the chicken mixture, then add the soy sauce, fish sauce and sugar, stirring well after each addition. Stir-fry for 2–3 minutes, or until the chicken is cooked through and the rice is piping hot.

Check the seasoning and, if necessary, add a little extra soy sauce. Turn the rice and chicken mixture into a warmed serving dish. Season lightly with black pepper and garnish with shredded spring onion and onion slices. Serve immediately.

Singapore Noodles

Serves 4

225 g/8 oz flat rice noodles
3 tbsp sunflower oil
2 shallots, peeled and sliced
2 garlic cloves, peeled and crushed
2 tbsp freshly grated root ginger
1 red pepper, deseeded and
finely sliced
1 hot red chilli, deseeded and
finely chopped
175 g/6 oz peeled raw prawns
125 g/4 oz boneless pork, diced
175 g/6 oz boneless
chicken, diced
1 tbsp curry powder
1 tsp each crushed fennel seeds
and ground cinnamon
50 g/2 oz frozen peas, thawed
juice of 1 lemon
3 tbsp fresh coriander leaves

Put the noodles into a large bowl and pour over boiling water to cover. Leave to stand for 3 minutes, or until slightly underdone according to the packet directions. Drain well and reserve.

Heat a wok until almost smoking. Add the oil and carefully swirl around to coat the sides of the wok. Add the shallots, garlic and ginger and cook for a few seconds. Add the pepper and chilli and stir-fry for 3–4 minutes, or until the pepper has softened.

Add the prawns, pork, chicken and curry powder to the wok. Stir-fry for a further 4–5 minutes until the meat and prawns are coloured on all sides. Then add the fennel seeds and the ground cinnamon and stir to mix.

Add the drained noodles to the wok along with the peas and cook for a further 1–2 minutes until heated through. Add the lemon juice to taste. Sprinkle with the fresh coriander leaves and serve immediately.

Pork Fried Noodles

Serves 4

125 g/4 oz dried thread egg noodles
125 g/4 oz broccoli florets
4 tbsp groundnut oil
350 g/12 oz pork tenderloin,
cut into slices
3 tbsp soy sauce
1 tbsp lemon juice
pinch granulated sugar
1 tsp chilli sauce
1 tbsp sesame oil
2.5 cm/1 inch piece fresh root ginger,
peeled and cut into sticks
1 garlic clove, peeled and chopped
1 green chilli, deseeded and sliced
125 g/4 oz mangetout, halved
2 medium eggs, lightly beaten
227 g can water chestnuts, drained
and sliced

To garnish:
radish rose
spring onion tassels

Place the noodles in a bowl and cover with boiling water. Leave to stand for 20 minutes, stirring occasionally, or until tender. Drain and reserve. Meanwhile, blanch the broccoli in a saucepan of lightly salted boiling water for 2 minutes. Drain, refresh under cold running water and reserve.

Heat a large wok or frying pan, add the groundnut oil and heat until just smoking. Add the pork and stir-fry for 5 minutes, or until browned. Using a slotted spoon, remove the pork slices and reserve.

Mix together the soy sauce, lemon juice, sugar, chilli sauce and sesame oil and reserve.

Add the ginger to the wok and stir-fry for 30 seconds. Add the garlic and chilli and stir-fry for 30 seconds. Add the reserved broccoli and stir-fry for 3 minutes. Stir in the mangetout, pork and reserved noodles with the beaten eggs and water chestnuts and stir-fry for 5 minutes or until heated through. Pour over the reserved chilli sauce, toss well and turn into a warmed serving dish. Garnish and serve immediately.

Chicken with Mango Tabbouleh

Serves 4

400 g/14 oz chicken breast fillet
200 ml/7 fl oz natural low fat yogurt
1 garlic clove, peeled and crushed
1 small red chilli, deseeded and
finely chopped
$^{1}/_{2}$ tsp ground turmeric
finely grated rind and juice
of $^{1}/_{2}$ lemon
fresh mint sprigs, to garnish

For the mango tabbouleh:
175 g/6 oz bulgur wheat
1 tsp olive oil
juice of $^{1}/_{2}$ lemon
$^{1}/_{2}$ red onion, finely chopped
1 ripe mango, halved, stoned,
peeled and chopped
$^{1}/_{4}$ cucumber, finely diced
2 tbsp freshly chopped parsley
2 tbsp freshly shredded mint
salt and finely ground black pepper

If using wooden skewers, pre-soak them in cold water for at least 30 minutes. (This stops them from burning during grilling.) Cut the chicken into five 1 cm/2 x $^{1}/_{2}$ inch strips and place in a shallow dish. Mix together the yogurt, garlic, chilli, turmeric, lemon rind and juice. Pour over the chicken and toss to coat. Cover and leave to marinate in the refrigerator for up to 8 hours.

To make the tabbouleh, put the bulgur wheat in a bowl. Pour over enough boiling water to cover. Put a plate over the bowl. Leave to soak for 20 minutes.

Whisk together the oil and lemon juice in a bowl. Add the red onion and leave to marinade for 10 minutes.

Drain the bulgur wheat and squeeze out any excess moisture in a clean tea towel. Add to the red onion with the mango, cucumber, herbs and season to taste with salt and pepper. Toss together.

Thread the chicken strips on to eight wooden or metal skewers. Cook under a hot grill for 8 minutes. Turn and brush with the marinade, until the chicken is lightly browned and cooked through. Spoon the tabbouleh on to individual plates. Arrange the chicken skewers on top and garnish with the sprigs of mint. Serve warm or cold.

Pork with Tofu & Coconut

Serves 4

50 g/2 oz unsalted cashew nuts
1 tbsp ground coriander
1 tbsp ground cumin
2 tsp hot chilli powder
2.5 cm/1 inch piece fresh root ginger,
peeled and chopped
1 tbsp oyster sauce
4 tbsp groundnut oil
400 ml/14 fl oz coconut milk
175 g/6 oz rice noodles
450 g/1 lb pork tenderloin,
thickly sliced
1 red chilli, deseeded and sliced
1 green chilli, deseeded and sliced
1 bunch spring onions, trimmed and
thickly sliced
3 tomatoes, roughly chopped
75 g/3 oz tofu, drained
2 tbsp freshly chopped coriander
2 tbsp freshly chopped mint
salt and freshly ground black pepper

Place the cashew nuts, coriander, cumin, chilli powder, ginger and oyster sauce in a food processor and blend until well ground. Heat a wok or large frying pan, add 2 tablespoons of the oil and when hot, add the cashew mixture and stir-fry for 1 minute. Stir in the coconut milk, bring to the boil, then simmer for 1 minute. Pour into a small jug and reserve. Wipe the wok clean.

Meanwhile, place the rice noodles in a bowl, cover with boiling water, leave to stand for 5 minutes, then drain thoroughly.

Reheat the wok, add the remaining oil and when hot, add the pork and stir-fry for 5 minutes or until browned all over. Add the chillies and spring onions and stir-fry for 2 minutes.

Add the tomatoes and tofu to the wok with the noodles and coconut mixture and stir-fry for a further 2 minutes, or until heated through, being careful not to break up the tofu. Sprinkle with the chopped coriander and mint, season to taste with salt and pepper and stir. Tip into a warmed serving dish and serve immediately.

Szechuan Beef

Serves 4

450 g/1 lb beef fillet
3 tbsp hoisin sauce
2 tbsp yellow bean sauce
2 tbsp dry sherry
1 tbsp brandy
2 tbsp groundnut oil
2 red chillies, deseeded and sliced
8 bunches spring onions, trimmed and chopped
2 garlic cloves, peeled and chopped
2.5 cm/1 inch piece fresh root ginger, peeled and cut into matchsticks
1 carrot, peeled, sliced lengthways and cut into short lengths
2 green peppers, deseeded and cut into 2.5 cm/1 inch pieces
227g can water chestnuts, drained and halved
fresh coriander sprigs, to garnish
freshly cooked noodles with freshly ground Szechuan peppercorns, to serve

Trim the beef, discarding any sinew or fat, then cut into 5 mm/¹/₄ inch strips. Place in a large shallow dish. In a bowl, stir the hoisin sauce, yellow bean sauce, sherry and brandy together until well blended. Pour over the beef and turn until coated evenly. Cover with clingfilm and leave to marinate for at least 30 minutes.

Heat a wok or large frying pan, add the oil and when hot, add the chillies, spring onions, garlic and ginger and stir-fry for 2 minutes or until softened. Using a slotted spoon, transfer to a plate and keep warm.

Add the carrot and peppers to the wok and stir-fry for 4 minutes or until slightly softened. Transfer to a plate and keep warm.

Drain the beef, reserving the marinade, add to the wok and stir-fry for 3–5 minutes or until browned. Return the chilli mixture, the carrot and pepper mixture and the marinade to the wok, add the water chestnuts and stir-fry for 2 minutes or until heated through. Garnish with coriander sprigs and serve immediately with the noodles.

Cashew ✎ Pork Stir Fry

Serves 4

450 g/1 lb pork tenderloin
4 tbsp soy sauce
1 tbsp cornflour
125 g/4 oz unsalted cashew nuts
4 tbsp sunflower oil
450 g/1 lb leeks, trimmed
and shredded
2.5 cm/1 inch piece fresh root ginger,
peeled and cut into matchsticks
2 garlic cloves, peeled and chopped
1 red pepper, deseeded and sliced
300 ml/$^{1}/_{2}$ pint chicken stock
2 tbsp freshly chopped coriander
freshly cooked noodles, to serve

Using a sharp knife, trim the pork, discarding any sinew or fat. Cut into 2 cm/3⁄4 inch slices and place in a shallow dish. Blend the soy sauce and cornflour together until smooth and free from lumps, then pour over the pork. Stir until coated in the cornflour mixture, then cover with clingfilm and leave to marinate in the refrigerator for at least 30 minutes.

Heat a nonstick frying pan until hot, add the cashew nuts and dry-fry for 2–3 minutes, or until toasted, stirring frequently. Transfer to a plate and reserve.

Heat a wok or large frying pan, add 2 tablespoons of the oil and when hot, add the leeks, ginger, garlic and pepper and stir-fry for 5 minutes or until softened. Using a slotted spoon, transfer to a plate and keep warm.

Drain the pork, reserving the marinade. Add the remaining oil to the wok and when hot, add the pork and stir-fry for 5 minutes or until browned. Return the reserved vegetables to the wok with the marinade and the stock. Bring to the boil, then simmer for 2 minutes, or until the sauce has thickened. Stir in the toasted cashew nuts and chopped coriander and serve immediately with freshly cooked noodles.

Pork with Yellow Bean Sauce

Serves 4

450 g/1 lb pork fillet
2 tbsp light soy sauce
2 tbsp orange juice
2 tsp cornflour
3 tbsp groundnut oil
2 garlic cloves, peeled and crushed
175 g/6 oz carrots, peeled and cut
into matchsticks
125 g/4 oz fine green beans,
trimmed and halved
2 spring onions, trimmed and cut
into strips
4 tbsp yellow bean sauce
1 tbsp freshly chopped flat leaf
parsley, to garnish
freshly cooked egg noodles,
to serve

Remove any fat or sinew from the pork fillet, and cut into thin strips. Blend the soy sauce, orange juice and cornflour in a bowl and mix thoroughly. Place the meat in a shallow dish, pour over the soy sauce mixture, cover and leave to marinate in the refrigerator for 1 hour. Drain with a slotted spoon, reserving the marinade.

Heat the wok, then add 2 tablespoons of the oil and stir-fry the pork with the garlic for 2 minutes, or until the meat is sealed. Remove with a slotted spoon and reserve.

Add the remaining oil to the wok and cook the carrots, beans and spring onions for about 3 minutes, until tender but still crisp. Return the pork to the wok with the reserved marinade, then pour over the yellow bean sauce. Stir-fry for a further 1–2 minutes, or until the pork is tender. Sprinkle with the chopped parsley and serve immediately with freshly cooked egg noodles.

Chilli Lamb

Serves 4

550 g/1¹/₄ lb lamb fillet
3 tbsp groundnut oil
1 large onion, peeled and
finely sliced
2 garlic cloves, peeled and crushed
4 tsp cornflour
4 tbsp hot chilli sauce
2 tbsp white wine vinegar
4 tsp dark soft brown sugar
1 tsp Chinese five spice powder
fresh coriander sprigs, to garnish

To serve:

freshly cooked noodles
4 tbsp Greek style yogurt

Trim the lamb fillet, discarding any fat or sinew, then place it on a clean chopping board and cut into thin strips. Heat a wok and pour in 2 tablespoons of the groundnut oil and when hot, stir-fry the lamb for 3–4 minutes, or until it is browned. Remove the lamb strips with their juices and reserve.

Add the remaining oil to the wok, then stir-fry the onion and garlic for 2 minutes, or until softened. Remove with a slotted spoon and add to the lamb.

Blend the cornflour with 125 ml/4 fl oz of cold water, then stir in the chilli sauce, vinegar, sugar and Chinese five spice powder. Pour this into the wok, turn up the heat and bring the mixture to the boil. Cook for 30 seconds or until the sauce thickens.

Return the lamb to the wok with the onion and garlic, stir thoroughly and heat through until piping hot. Garnish with fresh coriander sprigs and serve immediately with freshly cooked noodles, topped with a spoonful of Greek yogurt.

Shredded Beef in Hoisin Sauce

Serves 4

2 celery sticks
125 g/4 oz carrots
450 g/1 lb rump steak
2 tbsp cornflour
salt and freshly ground
black pepper
2 tbsp sunflower oil
4 spring onions, trimmed
and chopped
2 tbsp light soy sauce
1 tbsp hoisin sauce
1 tbsp sweet chilli sauce
2 tbsp dry sherry
250 g pack fine egg thread noodles
1 tbsp freshly chopped coriander

Trim the celery and peel the carrots, then cut into fine matchsticks and reserve.

Place the steak between two sheets of greaseproof paper or baking parchment. Beat the steak with a meat mallet or rolling pin until very thin, then slice into strips. Season the cornflour with salt and pepper and use to coat the steak. Reserve.

Heat a wok, add the oil and when hot, add the spring onions and cook for 1 minute, then add the steak and stir-fry for a further 3–4 minutes, or until the meat is sealed.

Add the celery and carrot matchsticks to the wok and stir-fry for a further 2 minutes before adding the soy, hoisin and chilli sauces and the sherry. Bring to the boil and simmer for 2–3 minutes, or until the steak is tender and the vegetables are cooked.

Plunge the fine egg noodles into boiling water and leave for 4 minutes. Drain, then spoon onto a large serving dish. Top with the cooked shredded steak, then sprinkle with chopped coriander and serve immediately.

Duck in Black Bean Sauce

Serves 4

450 g/1 lb duck breast, skinned
1 tbsp light soy sauce
1 tbsp Chinese rice wine or
dry sherry
2.5 cm/1 inch piece fresh root ginger
3 garlic cloves
2 spring onions
2 tbsp Chinese preserved
black beans
1 tbsp groundnut or vegetable oil
150 ml/^{1}/$_{4}$ pint chicken stock
shredded spring onions, to garnish
freshly cooked noodles, to serve

Using a sharp knife, trim the duck breasts, removing any fat. Slice thickly and place in a shallow dish. Mix together the soy sauce and Chinese rice wine or sherry and pour over the duck. Leave to marinate for 1 hour in the refrigerator, then drain and discard the marinade.

Peel the ginger and chop finely. Peel the garlic cloves and either chop finely or crush. Trim the root from the spring onions, discard the outer leaves and chop. Finely chop the black beans.

Heat a wok or large frying pan, add the oil and when very hot, add the ginger, garlic, spring onions and black beans and stir-fry for 30 seconds. Add the drained duck and stir-fry for 3–5 minutes or until the duck is browned.

Add the chicken stock to the wok, bring to the boil, then reduce the heat and simmer for 5 minutes, or until the duck is cooked and the sauce is reduced and thickened. Remove from the heat. Tip on to a bed of freshly cooked noodles, garnish with spring onion shreds and serve immediately.

Chicken Chow Mein

Serves 4

225 g/8 oz egg noodles
5 tsp sesame oil
4 tsp light soy sauce
2 tbsp Chinese rice wine or
dry sherry
salt and freshly ground black pepper
225 g/8 oz skinless chicken breast
fillets, cut into strips
3 tbsp groundnut oil
2 garlic cloves, peeled and
finely chopped
50 g/2 oz mangetout peas,
finely sliced
50 g/2 oz cooked ham, cut into
fine strips
2 tsp dark soy sauce
pinch granulated sugar

To garnish:

shredded spring onions
toasted sesame seeds

Bring a large saucepan of water to the boil and add the noodles. Cook for 3–5 minutes, drain and plunge into cold water. Drain again, add 1 tablespoon of the sesame oil and stir lightly.

Place 2 teaspoons of light soy sauce, 1 tablespoon of Chinese rice wine or sherry, and 1 teaspoon of the sesame oil, with seasoning to taste in a bowl. Add the chicken and stir well. Cover lightly and leave to marinate in the refrigerator for about 15 minutes.

Heat the wok over a high heat, add 1 tablespoon of the groundnut oil and when very hot, add the chicken and its marinade and stir-fry for 2 minutes. Remove the chicken and juices and reserve. Wipe the wok clean with absorbent kitchen paper. Reheat the wok and add the oil. Add the garlic and toss in the oil for 20 seconds. Add the mangetout peas and the ham and stir-fry for 1 minute. Add the noodles, remaining light soy sauce, Chinese rice wine or sherry, the dark soy sauce and sugar. Season to taste with salt and pepper and stir-fry for 2 minutes.

Add the chicken and juices to the wok and stir-fry for 4 minutes, or until the chicken is cooked. Drizzle over the remaining sesame oil. Garnish with spring onions and sesame seeds and serve.

Szechuan Turkey Noodles

Serves 4

1 tbsp tomato paste
2 tsp black bean sauce
2 tsp cider vinegar
salt and freshly ground black pepper
$^1/_2$ tsp Szechuan pepper
2 tsp caster sugar
4 tsp sesame oil
225 g/8 oz dried egg noodles
2 tbsp groundnut oil
2 tsp freshly grated root ginger
3 garlic cloves, peeled and
roughly chopped
2 shallots, peeled and
finely chopped
2 courgettes, trimmed and cut into
fine matchsticks
450 g/1 lb turkey breast, skinned
and cut into strips
deep-fried onion rings, to garnish

Mix together the tomato paste, black bean sauce, cider vinegar, pinch salt and pepper, the sugar and half the sesame oil. Chill in the refrigerator for 30 minutes.

Bring a large saucepan of lightly salted water to the boil and add the noodles. Cook for 3–5 minutes, drain and plunge immediately into cold water. Toss with the remaining sesame oil and reserve.

Heat the wok until very hot, then add the oil and when hot, add the ginger, garlic and shallots. Stir-fry for 20 seconds, then add the courgettes and turkey strips. Stir-fry for 3–4 minutes, or until the turkey strips are sealed.

Add the prepared chilled black bean sauce and continue to stir-fry for another 4 minutes over a high heat. Add the drained noodles to the wok and stir until the noodles, turkey, vegetables and the sauce are well mixed together. Garnish with the deep-fried onion rings and serve immediately.

Lamb with Stir-fried Vegetables

Serves 4

550 g/1¹⁄₄ lb lamb fillet, cut into strips
2.5 cm/1 inch piece fresh root ginger,
peeled and cut into matchsticks
2 garlic cloves, peeled and chopped
4 tbsp soy sauce
2 tbsp dry sherry
2 tsp cornflour
4 tbsp groundnut oil
75 g/3 oz French beans, trimmed
and cut in half
2 medium carrots, peeled and cut
into matchsticks
1 red pepper, deseeded and cut
into chunks
1 yellow pepper, deseeded and cut
into chunks
225 g can water chestnuts, drained
and halved
3 tomatoes, chopped
freshly cooked sticky rice in banana
leaves, to serve (optional)

Place the lamb strips in a shallow dish. Mix together the ginger and half the garlic in a small bowl. Pour over the soy sauce and sherry and stir well. Pour over the lamb and stir until coated lightly. Cover with clingfilm and leave to marinate for at least 30 minutes, occasionally spooning the marinade over the lamb.

Using a slotted spoon, lift the lamb from the marinade and place on a plate. Blend the cornflour and the marinade together until smooth and reserve.

Heat a wok or large frying pan, add 2 tablespoons of the oil and when hot, add the remaining garlic, French beans, carrots and peppers and stir-fry for 5 minutes. Using a slotted spoon, transfer the vegetables to a plate and keep warm.

Heat the remaining oil in the wok, add the lamb and stir-fry for 2 minutes or until tender. Return the vegetables to the wok with the water chestnuts, tomatoes and reserved marinade mixture. Bring to the boil then simmer for 1 minute. Serve immediately with freshly cooked sticky rice in banana leaves, if liked.

Pork in Peanut Sauce

Serves 4

450 g/1 lb pork fillet
2 tbsp light soy sauce
1 tbsp vinegar
1 tsp caster sugar
1 tsp Chinese five spice powder
2–4 garlic cloves, peeled
and crushed
2 tbsp groundnut oil
1 large onion, peeled and
finely sliced
125 g/4 oz carrots, peeled and cut
into matchsticks
2 celery sticks, trimmed and sliced
125 g/4 oz French beans, trimmed
and halved
3 tbsp smooth peanut butter
1 tbsp freshly chopped flat
leaf parsley

To serve:

freshly cooked basmati and wild rice
green salad

Remove any fat or sinew from the pork fillet, cut into thin strips and reserve. Blend the soy sauce, vinegar, sugar, Chinese five spice powder and garlic in a bowl and add the pork. Cover and leave to marinate in the refrigerator for at least 30 minutes.

Drain the pork, reserving any marinade. Heat the wok, then add the oil and, when hot, stir-fry the pork for 3–4 minutes, or until sealed.

Add the onion, carrots, celery and beans to the wok and stir-fry for 4–5 minutes, or until the meat is tender and the vegetables are softened.

Blend the reserved marinade, the peanut butter and 2 tablespoons of hot water together. When smooth, stir into the wok and cook for several minutes more until the sauce is thick and the pork is piping hot. Sprinkle with the chopped parsley and serve immediately with the basmati and wild rice and a green salad.

Fried Rice with Chilli Beef

Serves 4

225 g/8 oz beef fillet
375 g/12 oz long-grain rice
4 tbsp groundnut oil
3 onions, peeled and thinly sliced
2 hot red chillies, deseeded and
finely chopped
2 tbsp light soy sauce
2 tsp tomato paste
salt and freshly ground
black pepper
2 tbsp milk
2 tbsp flour
15 g/ $^{1}/_{2}$ oz butter
2 medium eggs

Trim the beef fillet, discarding any fat, then cut into thin strips and reserve. Cook the rice in boiling salted water for 15 minutes or according to packet directions, then drain and reserve.

Heat a wok and add 3 tablespoons of oil. When hot, add 2 of the sliced onions and stir-fry for 2–3 minutes. Add the beef to the wok, together with the chillies, and stir-fry for a further 3 minutes, or until tender.

Add the rice to the wok with the soy sauce and tomato paste. Stir-fry for 1–2 minutes, or until piping hot. Season to taste with salt and pepper and keep warm. Meanwhile, toss the remaining onion in the milk, then the flour in batches. In a small frying pan fry the onion in the last 1 tablespoon of oil until crisp, then reserve.

Melt the butter in a small omelette pan. Beat the eggs with 2 teaspoons of water and pour into the pan. Cook gently, stirring frequently, until the egg has set, forming an omelette, then slide onto a clean chopping board and cut into thin strips. Add to the fried rice, sprinkle with the crispy onion and serve immediately.

Fish 🙠
Vegetables

꧁

Originating in countries and islands with stretches of sun-kissed coastline, it is no surprise that there are many street food recipes featuring fresh seafood. Recreate the exotic by cooking up some Hot Prawn Noodles or Coconut Seafood, both ready in no time. If it's a vegetable dish you're after, try the Huevos Rancheros, a traditional Mexican breakfast wrapped in tortillas, bursting with flavour to kick start your day.

Sweet & Sour Prawns with Noodles

Serves 4

425 g can pineapple pieces in natural juice
1 green pepper, deseeded and cut into quarters
1 tbsp groundnut oil
1 onion, cut into thin wedges
3 tbsp soft brown sugar
150 ml/$\frac{1}{4}$ pint chicken stock
4 tbsp wine vinegar
1 tbsp tomato purée
1 tbsp light soy sauce
1 tbsp cornflour
350 g/12 oz raw tiger prawns, peeled
225 g/8 oz pak choi, shredded
350 g/12 oz medium egg noodles
coriander leaves, to garnish

Drain the pineapple and reserve 2 tablespoons of the juice. Remove the membrane from the quartered peppers and cut into thin strips.

Heat the oil in a saucepan. Add the onion and pepper and cook for about 4 minutes or until the onion has softened.

Add the pineapple, the sugar, stock, vinegar, tomato purée and the soy sauce. Bring the sauce to the boil and simmer for about 4 minutes.

Blend the cornflour with the reserved pineapple juice and stir into the pan, stirring until thickened.

Clean the prawns if needed. Wash the pak choi thoroughly, then shred. Add the prawns and pak choi to the sauce. Simmer gently for 3 minutes or until the prawns are cooked and have turned pink.

Cook the noodles in boiling water for 4–5 minutes until just tender. Drain and arrange the noodles on a warmed plate and pour over the sweet-and-sour prawns. Garnish with coriander leaves and serve immediately.

Hot Prawn Noodles

Serves 4

600 ml/1 pint vegetable stock
350 g/12 oz Chinese egg noodles
1 tbsp sunflower oil
1 garlic clove, peeled and very
finely chopped
1 red chilli, deseeded and
finely chopped
3 tbsp sesame seeds
3 tbsp dark soy sauce
2 tbsp sesame oil
175 g/6 oz shelled cooked prawns
3 tbsp freshly chopped coriander
freshly ground black pepper
fresh coriander sprigs, to garnish

Pour the vegetable stock into a large saucepan and bring to the boil. Add the egg noodles, stir once, then cook according to the packet instructions, usually about 3 minutes.

Meanwhile, heat the sunflower oil in a small frying pan. Add the chopped garlic and chilli and cook gently for a few seconds. Add the sesame seeds and cook, stirring continuously, for 1 minute, or until golden.

Add the soy sauce, sesame oil and prawns to the frying pan. Continue cooking for a few seconds, until the mixture is just starting to bubble, then remove immediately from the heat.

Drain the noodles thoroughly and return to the pan. Add the prawns in the dressing mixture, and the chopped coriander and season to taste with black pepper. Toss gently to coat the noodles with the hot dressing.

Tip into a warmed serving bowl or spoon on to individual plates and serve immediately, garnished with sprigs of fresh coriander.

Crispy Prawn Stir Fry

Serves 4

3 tbsp soy sauce
1 tsp cornflour
pinch of caster sugar
6 tbsp groundnut oil
450 g/1 lb raw shelled tiger prawns,
halved lengthways
125 g/4 oz carrots, peeled and cut
into matchsticks
2.5 cm/1 inch piece fresh root
ginger, peeled and cut into
matchsticks
125 g/4 oz mangetout peas,
trimmed and shredded
125 g/4 oz asparagus spears, cut
into short lengths
125 g/4 oz beansprouts
1/4 head Chinese leaves, shredded
2 tsp sesame oil

Mix together the soy sauce, cornflour and sugar in a small bowl and reserve.

Heat a large wok, then add 3 tablespoons of the oil and heat until almost smoking. Add the prawns and stir-fry for 4 minutes, or until pink all over. Using a slotted spoon, transfer the prawns to a plate and keep warm in a low oven.

Add the remaining oil to the wok and when just smoking, add the carrots and ginger and stir-fry for 1 minute, or until slightly softened, then add the mangetout peas and stir-fry for a further 1 minute. Add the asparagus and stir-fry for 4 minutes, or until softened.

Add the beansprouts and Chinese leaves and stir-fry for 2 minutes, or until the leaves are slightly wilted. Pour in the soy sauce mixture and return the prawns to the wok. Stir-fry over a medium heat until piping hot, then add the sesame oil, give a final stir and serve immediately.

Scallops with Black Bean Sauce

Serves 4

700 g/1¹/2 lb scallops, with
their coral
2 tbsp vegetable oil
2–3 tbsp Chinese fermented black
beans, rinsed, drained and
coarsely chopped
2 garlic cloves, peeled and
finely chopped
4 cm/1¹/2 inch piece fresh root ginger,
peeled and finely chopped
4–5 spring onions, thinly
sliced diagonally
2–3 tbsp soy sauce
1¹/2 tbsp Chinese rice wine or
dry sherry
1–2 tsp granulated sugar
1 tbsp fish stock or water
2–3 dashes hot pepper sauce
1 tbsp sesame oil
freshly cooked noodles, to serve

Pat the scallops dry with absorbent kitchen paper. Carefully separate the orange coral from the scallop. Peel off and discard the membrane and thickish opaque muscle that attaches the coral to the scallop. Cut any large scallops crossways in half, leave the corals whole.

Heat a wok or large frying pan, add the oil and when hot, add the white scallop meat and stir-fry for 2 minutes, or until just beginning to colour on the edges. Using a slotted spoon or spatula, transfer to a plate. Reserve.

Add the black beans, garlic and ginger and stir-fry for 1 minute. Add the spring onions, soy sauce, Chinese rice wine or sherry, sugar, fish stock or water, hot pepper sauce and the corals and stir until mixed.

Return the scallops and juices to the wok and stir-fry gently for 3 minutes, or until the scallops and corals are cooked through. Add a little more stock or water if necessary. Stir in the sesame oil and turn into a heated serving dish. Serve immediately with noodles.

Fish Balls in Yellow Bean Sauce

Serves 4

450 g/1 lb skinless white fish fillets,
such as cod or haddock,
cut into pieces
$^1/_2$ tsp salt
1 tbsp cornflour
2 spring onions, trimmed
and chopped
1 tbsp freshly chopped coriander
1 tsp soy sauce
1 medium egg white
freshly ground black pepper
tarragon sprigs, to garnish
freshly cooked rice, to serve

For the yellow bean sauce:

75 ml/3 fl oz fish or chicken stock
1–2 tsp yellow bean sauce
2 tbsp soy sauce
1–2 tbsp Chinese rice wine or
dry sherry
1 tsp chilli bean sauce, or to taste
1 tsp sesame oil
1 tsp granulated sugar (optional)

Put the fish pieces, salt, cornflour, spring onions, coriander, soy sauce and egg white into a food processor, season to taste with pepper, then blend until a smooth paste forms, scraping down the sides of the bowl occasionally.

With dampened hands, shape the mixture into 2.5 cm/1 inch balls. Transfer to a baking tray and chill in the refrigerator for at least 30 minutes.

Bring a large saucepan of water to simmering point. Working in two or three batches, drop in the fish balls and poach gently for 3–4 minutes or until they float to the top. Transfer to absorbent kitchen paper to drain.

Put all the sauce ingredients in a wok or large frying pan and bring to the boil. Add the fish balls to the sauce and stir-fry gently for 2–3 minutes until piping hot. Transfer to a warmed serving dish, garnish with tarragon sprigs and serve immediately with freshly cooked rice.

Battered Cod & Chunky Chips

Serves 4

15 g/¹/₂ oz fresh yeast
300 ml/¹/₂ pint beer
225 g/8 oz plain flour
1 tsp salt
700 g/1¹/₂ lb potatoes
450 ml/³/₄ pint groundnut oil
4 cod fillets, about 225 g/8 oz each,
skinned and boned
2 tbsp seasoned plain flour

To garnish:

lemon wedges
flat-leaf parsley sprigs

To serve:

tomato ketchup
vinegar

Dissolve the yeast with a little of the beer in a jug and mix to a paste. Pour in the remaining beer, whisking all the time until smooth. Place the flour and salt in a bowl, and gradually pour in the beer mixture, whisking continuously to make a thick smooth batter. Cover the bowl and allow the batter to stand at room temperature for 1 hour.

Peel the potatoes and cut into thick slices. Cut each slice lengthways to make chunky chips. Place them in a non-stick frying pan and heat, shaking the pan until all the moisture has evaporated. Turn them onto absorbent kitchen paper to dry off.

Heat the oil to 180˚C/350˚F, then fry the chips a few at a time for 4–5 minutes until crisp and golden. Drain on absorbent kitchen paper and keep warm.

Pat the cod fillets dry, then coat in the flour. Dip the floured fillets into the reserved batter. Fry for 2–3 minutes until cooked and crisp, then drain. Garnish with lemon wedges and parsley and serve immediately with the chips, tomato ketchup and vinegar.

Plaice Nuggets with Tartare Sauce

Serves 4

75 g/3 oz fresh white breadcrumbs
3 tbsp freshly grated
Parmesan cheese
salt and freshly ground black pepper
1 tbsp dried oregano
1 medium egg
450 g/1 lb plaice fillets
300 ml/^{1}/$_2$ pint vegetable oil for
deep frying
fat chips, to serve

For the tartare sauce:

200 ml/7 fl oz prepared mayonnaise
50 g/2 oz gherkins, finely chopped
2 tbsp freshly snipped chives
1 garlic clove, peeled and crushed
2–3 tbsp capers, drained
and chopped
pinch of cayenne pepper
sunflower oil for deep frying

Mix together the breadcrumbs, Parmesan cheese, seasoning and oregano on a large plate. Lightly beat the egg in a shallow dish. Then, using a sharp knife, cut the plaice fillets into thick strips. Coat the plaice strips in the beaten egg, allowing any excess to drip back into the dish, then dip the strips into the breadcrumbs until well coated. Place the goujons on a baking sheet, cover and chill in the refrigerator for 30 minutes.

Meanwhile, to make the tartare sauce, mix together the mayonnaise, gherkins, chives, garlic, capers and cayenne pepper. Stir, then season to taste with salt and pepper. Place in a bowl, cover loosely and store in the refrigerator until required.

Pour the oil into a large wok. Heat to 190°C/375°F, or until a small cube of bread turns golden and crisp in about 30 seconds. Cook the plaice goujons in batches for about 4 minutes, turning occasionally, until golden. Using a slotted spoon, remove and drain on absorbent kitchen paper. Serve immediately with the tartare sauce and chips.

Salmon Teriyaki with Noodles

Serves 4

350 g/12 oz salmon fillet
3 tbsp Japanese soy sauce
3 tbsp mirin or sweet sherry
3 tbsp sake
1 tbsp freshly grated root ginger
225 g/8 oz spring greens
groundnut oil for deep-frying
pinch salt
$^1/_2$ tsp caster sugar
125 g/4 oz cellophane noodles

To garnish:

1 tbsp freshly chopped dill
fresh dill sprigs
zest of $^1/_2$ lemon

Cut the salmon into paper-thin slices and place in a shallow dish. Mix together the soy sauce, mirin or sherry, sake and the ginger. Pour over the salmon, cover and leave to marinate for 15–30 minutes.

Remove and discard the thick stalks from the greens. Lay several leaves on top of each other, roll up tightly, then shred finely. Pour in enough oil to cover about 5 cm/2 inches of the wok. Deep-fry the greens in batches for about 1 minute each until crisp. Remove and drain on absorbent kitchen paper. Transfer to a serving dish, sprinkle with salt and sugar and toss.

Place the noodles in a bowl and cover with warm water. Leave to soak for 15–20 minutes until soft, then drain. Snip into 15 cm/6 inch lengths.

Preheat the grill. Remove the salmon slices from the marinade, reserving the marinade for later, and arrange them in a single layer on a baking sheet. Grill for about 2 minutes, until lightly cooked, without turning.

When the oil in the wok is cool enough, tip most of it away, leaving about 1 tablespoon behind. Heat until hot, then add the noodles and the reserved marinade and stir-fry for 3–4 minutes. Tip the noodles into a large warmed serving bowl and arrange the salmon slices on top, garnished with chopped dill, fresh dill sprigs and lemon zest. Scatter with a little of the crispy greens and serve the rest separately.

Nasi Goreng

Serves 4

7 large shallots, peeled
1 red chilli, deseeded and
roughly chopped
2 garlic cloves, peeled and
roughly chopped
2 tsp each tomato purée and
Indonesian sweet soy sauce
(katjap manis)
4 tbsp sunflower oil
225 g/8 oz long-grain white rice
125 g/4 oz French beans, trimmed
3 medium eggs, beaten
pinch caster sugar
salt and freshly ground black pepper
225 g/8 oz cooked ham, shredded
225 g/8 oz cooked peeled prawns,
thawed if frozen
6 spring onions, trimmed and
thinly sliced
1 tbsp light soy sauce
3 tbsp freshly chopped coriander

Roughly chop 1 of the shallots and place with the chilli, garlic, tomato purée, sweet soy sauce and 1 tablespoon of the oil in a food processor and blend until smooth. Reserve. Boil the rice in salted water for 6–7 minutes until tender, adding the beans after 4 minutes. Drain and cool.

Beat the eggs with the sugar and a little salt and pepper. Heat a little of the oil in a small non-stick frying pan and add about one third of the egg mixture. Swirl to coat the base of the pan thinly and cook for about 1 minute until golden. Flip and cook the other side briefly before removing from the pan. Roll the omelette and slice thinly into strips. Repeat with the remaining egg to make 3 omelettes.

Thinly slice the rest of the shallots then heat 2 tablespoons of the oil in a clean frying pan. Cook the shallots for 8–10 minutes over a medium heat until golden and crisp. Drain on absorbent kitchen paper. Reserve.

Add the remaining tablespoon of oil to a large wok or frying pan and fry the chilli paste over a medium heat for 1 minute. Add the cooked rice and beans and stir-fry for 2 minutes. Add the ham and prawns and continue for a further 1–2 minutes. Add the omelette slices, half the fried shallots, the spring onions, soy sauce and chopped coriander. Stir-fry for a further minute until heated through. Spoon onto plates and garnish with the remaining crispy shallots. Serve immediately.

Red Prawn Curry

Serves 4

¹/₂ tbsp coriander seeds; 1 tsp cumin seeds; 1 tsp black peppercorns; ¹/₂ tsp salt; 1–2 dried red chillies; 2 shallots, peeled and chopped; 3–4 garlic cloves; 2.5 cm/1 inch piece fresh galangal or root ginger, peeled and chopped; 1 kaffir lime leaf or 1 tsp kaffir lime rind; ¹/₂ tsp red chilli powder; ¹/₂ tbsp shrimp paste; 1–1¹/₂ lemon grass stalks, outer leaves removed and thinly sliced; 750 ml/1¹/₄ pints coconut milk; 1 red chilli deseeded and thinly sliced; 2 tbsp Thai fish sauce; 2 tsp soft brown sugar; 1 red pepper, deseeded and thinly sliced; 550 g/1¹/₄ lb large peeled tiger prawns; 2 fresh lime leaves, shredded (optional); 2 tbsp fresh mint leaves, shredded 2 tbsp Thai or Italian basil leaves, shredded; freshly cooked Thai fragrant rice, to serve

Using a pestle and mortar or a spice grinder, grind the coriander and cumin seeds, peppercorns and salt to a fine powder. Add the dried chillies one at a time and grind to a fine powder.

Place the shallots, garlic, galangal or ginger, kaffir lime leaf or rind, chilli powder and shrimp paste in a food processor. Add the ground spices and process until a thick paste forms. Scrape down the bowl once or twice, adding a few drops of water if the mixture is too thick and not forming a paste. Stir in the lemon grass.

Transfer the paste to a large wok and cook over a medium heat for 2–3 minutes or until fragrant.

Stir in the coconut milk, bring to the boil, then lower the heat and simmer for about 10 minutes. Add the chilli, fish sauce, sugar and red pepper and simmer for 15 minutes.

Stir in the prawns and cook for 5 minutes, or until the prawns are pink and tender. Stir in the shredded herbs, heat for a further minute and serve immediately with the cooked rice.

Coconut Seafood

Serves 4

2 tbsp groundnut oil
450 g/1 lb raw king prawns, peeled
2 bunches spring onions, trimmed
and thickly sliced
1 garlic clove, peeled and chopped
2.5 cm/1 inch piece fresh root ginger,
peeled and cut into matchsticks
125 g/4 oz fresh shiitake mushrooms,
rinsed and halved
150 ml/$^1/_4$ pint dry white wine
200 ml/7 fl oz carton coconut cream
4 tbsp freshly chopped coriander
salt and freshly ground
black pepper
freshly cooked fragrant Thai rice

Heat a large wok, add the oil and heat until it is almost smoking, swirling the oil around the wok to coat the sides. Add the prawns and stir-fry over a high heat for 4-5 minutes, or until browned on all sides. Using a slotted spoon, transfer the prawns to a plate and keep warm in a low oven.

Add the spring onions, garlic and ginger to the wok and stir-fry for 1 minute. Add the mushrooms and stir-fry for a further 3 minutes. Using a slotted spoon, transfer the mushroom mixture to a plate and keep warm in a low oven.

Add the wine and coconut cream to the wok, bring to the boil and boil rapidly for 4 minutes, until reduced slightly.

Return the mushroom mixture and prawns to the wok, bring back to the boil, then simmer for 1 minute, stirring occasionally, until piping hot. Stir in the freshly chopped coriander and season to taste with salt and pepper. Serve immediately with the freshly cooked fragrant Thai rice.

Spicy Cod Rice

Serves 4

1 tbsp plain flour
1 tbsp freshly chopped coriander
1 tsp ground cumin
1 tsp ground coriander
550 g/1¼ lb thick-cut cod fillet, skinned and cut into large chunks
4 tbsp groundnut oil
50 g/2 oz cashew nuts
1 bunch spring onions, trimmed and diagonally sliced
1 red chilli, deseeded and chopped
1 carrot, peeled and cut into matchsticks
125 g/4 oz frozen peas
450 g/1 lb cooked long-grain rice
2 tbsp sweet chilli sauce
2 tbsp soy sauce

Mix together the flour, coriander, cumin and ground coriander on a large plate. Coat the cod in the spice mixture then place on a baking sheet, cover and chill in the refrigerator for 30 minutes.

Heat a large wok, then add 2 tablespoons of the oil and heat until almost smoking. Stir-fry the cashew nuts for 1 minute, until browned, then remove and reserve.

Add a further 1 tablespoon of the oil and heat until almost smoking. Add the cod and stir-fry for 2 minutes. Using a fish slice, turn the cod pieces over and cook for a further 2 minutes, until golden. Remove from the wok, place on a warm plate, cover and keep warm.

Add the remaining oil to the wok, heat until almost smoking then stir-fry the spring onions and chilli for 1 minute before adding the carrots and peas and stir-frying for a further 2 minutes. Stir in the rice, chilli sauce, soy sauce and cashew nuts and stir-fry for 3 more minutes. Add the cod, heat for 1 minute, then serve immediately.

Royal Fried Rice

Serves 4

450 g/1 lb Thai fragrant rice
2 large eggs
2 tsp sesame oil
salt and freshly ground black pepper
3 tbsp vegetable oil
1 red pepper, deseeded and
finely diced
1 yellow and 1 green pepper,
deseeded and finely diced
2 red onions, peeled and diced
125 g/4 oz sweetcorn kernels
125 g/4 oz cooked peeled prawns,
thawed if frozen
125 g/4 oz white crabmeat,
drained if canned
1/4 tsp caster sugar
2 tsp light soy sauce

To garnish:
radish roses
freshly snipped and whole
chive leaves

Place the rice in a sieve, rinse with cold water, then drain. Place in a saucepan and add twice the volume of water, stirring briefly. Bring to the boil, cover and simmer gently for 15 minutes without further stirring. If the rice has fully absorbed the water while covered, add a little more water. Continue to simmer, uncovered, for another 5 minutes, or until the rice is fully cooked and the water has evaporated. Leave to cool.

Place the eggs, sesame oil and pinch salt in a small bowl. Using a fork, mix just to break the egg. Reserve.

Heat a wok and add 1 tablespoon of the vegetable oil. When very hot, stir-fry the peppers, onion and sweetcorn for 2 minutes or until the onion is soft. Remove the vegetables and reserve.

Clean the wok and add the remaining oil. When very hot, add the cold cooked rice and stir-fry for 3 minutes, or until it is heated through. Drizzle in the egg mixture and continue to stir-fry for 2–3 minutes or until the eggs have set.

Add the prawns and crabmeat to the rice. Stir-fry for 1 minute. Season to taste with salt and pepper and add the sugar with the soy sauce. Stir to mix and spoon into a warmed serving dish. Garnish with a radish flower and sprinkle with freshly snipped and whole chives. Serve immediately.

Thai Noodles with Tofu ⓥ

Serves 4

225 g/8 oz firm tofu
2 tbsp soy sauce
rind of 1 lime, grated
2 lemon grass stalks
1 red chilli
1 litre/1³/₄ pint vegetable stock
2 slices fresh root ginger, peeled
2 garlic cloves, peeled
2 sprigs of fresh coriander
175 g/6 oz dried thread egg noodles
125 g/4 oz shiitake or button mushrooms, sliced if large
2 carrots, peeled and cut into matchsticks
125 g/4 oz mangetout
125 g/4 oz bok choy or other Chinese leaf
1 tbsp freshly chopped coriander
salt and freshly ground black pepper
coriander sprigs, to garnish

Drain the tofu well and cut into cubes. Put into a shallow dish with the soy sauce and lime rind. Stir well to coat and leave to marinate for 30 minutes.

Meanwhile, put the lemon grass and chilli on a chopping board and bruise with the side of a large knife, ensuring the blade is pointing away from you. Put the vegetable stock in a large saucepan and add the lemon grass, chilli, ginger, garlic, and coriander. Bring to the boil, cover and simmer gently for 20 minutes.

Strain the stock into a clean pan. Return to the boil and add the noodles, tofu and its marinade and the mushrooms. Simmer gently for 4 minutes.

Add the carrots, mangetout, bok choy, coriander and simmer for a further 3–4 minutes until the vegetables are just tender. Season to taste with salt and pepper. Garnish with coriander sprigs. Serve immediately.

Spiced Tomato Pilau ⓥ

Serves 2–3

225 g/8 oz basmati rice
40 g/1½ oz unsalted butter
4 green cardamom pods
2 star anise
4 whole cloves
10 black peppercorns
5 cm/2 inch piece cinnamon stick
1 large red onion, peeled and finely sliced
175 g/6 oz canned chopped tomatoes
salt and freshly ground black pepper
fresh coriander sprigs, to garnish

Wash the rice in several changes of water until the water remains relatively clear. Drain the rice and cover with fresh water. Leave to soak for 30 minutes. Drain well and reserve.

Heat the wok, then melt the butter and add the cardamoms, star anise, cloves, black peppercorns and the cinnamon stick. Cook gently for 30 seconds. Increase the heat and add the onion. Stir-fry for 7–8 minutes until tender and starting to brown. Add the drained rice and cook a further 2–3 minutes.

Sieve the tomatoes and mix with sufficient warm water to make 450 ml/16 fl oz. Pour this into the wok, season to taste with salt and pepper and bring to the boil.

Cover, reduce the heat to very low and cook for 10 minutes. Remove the wok from the heat and leave covered for a further 10 minutes. Do not lift the lid during cooking or resting. Finally, uncover and mix well with a fork, heat for 1 minute, then garnish with the sprigs of fresh coriander and serve immediately.

Cold Sesame Noodles Ⓥ

Serves 4–8

450 g/1 lb buckwheat (soba)
noodles or wholewheat spaghetti
pinch salt
1 tbsp each sesame and groundnut oil
1 green pepper, deseeded and
thinly sliced
125 g/4 oz daikon (mooli),
cut into julienne strips
125 g/4 oz mangetout or green
beans, trimmed and sliced
2 garlic cloves, peeled and
finely chopped
2 tbsp soy sauce, or to taste
1 tbsp cider vinegar
2 tbsp sweet chilli sauce, or to taste
2 tsp granulated sugar
75 g/3 oz peanut butter
6–8 spring onions, trimmed and
diagonally sliced

To garnish:

toasted sesame seeds
julienne strips of cucumber

Bring a large pan of lightly salted water to a rolling boil. Add the noodles or spaghetti and cook according to the packet instructions, or until 'al dente'. Drain, rinse and drain again, then toss in the sesame oil and reserve.

Heat the groundnut oil in a wok or large frying pan over a high heat. Add the green pepper, daikon and mangetout or green beans and stir-fry for 1 minute. Stir in the garlic and cook for 30 seconds.

Add the soy sauce to the pan with the vinegar, chilli sauce, sugar, peanut butter and 50 ml/2 fl oz of hot water. Simmer, stirring constantly, until the peanut butter is smooth, adding a little more water if necessary and adjusting the seasoning to taste.

Add the spring onions and the reserved noodles or spaghetti to the peanut sauce and cook, stirring, for 2–3 minutes, or until heated through. Tip the mixture into a large serving bowl and allow to cool to room temperature, stirring occasionally. Garnish with the toasted sesame seeds and cucumber julienne strips before serving.

Courgette & Tarragon Tortilla Ⓥ

Serves 2–6

700 g/1½ lb potatoes
3 tbsp olive oil
1 onion, peeled and thinly sliced
salt and freshly ground
black pepper
1 courgette, trimmed and
thinly sliced
6 medium eggs
2 tbsp freshly chopped tarragon
tomato wedges, to serve

Peel the potatoes and thinly slice. Dry the slices in a clean tea towel to get them as dry as possible. Heat the oil in a large heavy-based pan, add the onion and cook for 3 minutes. Add the potatoes with a little salt and pepper, then stir the potatoes and onion lightly to coat in the oil.

Reduce the heat to the lowest possible setting, cover and cook gently for 5 minutes. Turn the potatoes and onion over and continue to cook for a further 5 minutes. Give the pan a shake every now and again to ensure that the potatoes do not stick to the base or burn. Add the courgette, then cover and cook for a further 10 minutes.

Beat the eggs and tarragon together and season to taste with salt and pepper. Pour the egg mixture over the vegetables and return to the heat. Cook on a low heat for up to 20–25 minutes, or until there is no liquid egg left on the surface of the tortilla.

Turn the tortilla over by inverting the tortilla onto the lid or onto a flat plate. Return the pan to the heat and cook for a final 3–5 minutes, or until the underside is golden brown. If preferred, place the tortilla under a preheated grill for 4 minutes, or until set and golden brown on top. Cut into small squares and serve hot or cold with tomato wedges.

Rice ❧ Papaya Salad

Serves 4

175 g/6 oz easy-cook basmati rice
1 cinnamon stick, bruised
1 bird's-eye chilli, deseeded and finely chopped
rind and juice of 2 limes
rind and juice of 2 lemons
2 tbsp Thai fish sauce (or vegetarian oyster sauce or soy sauce)
1 tbsp soft light brown sugar
1 papaya, peeled and seeds removed
1 mango, peeled and stone removed
1 green chilli, deseeded and finely chopped
2 tbsp freshly chopped coriander
1 tbsp freshly chopped mint
250 g/9 oz cooked chicken
50 g/2 oz roasted peanuts, chopped
strips of pitta bread, to serve

Rinse and drain the rice and pour into a saucepan. Add 450 ml/$^3/_4$ pint boiling salted water and the cinnamon stick. Bring to the boil, reduce the heat to a very low heat, cover and cook without stirring for 15–18 minutes, or until all the liquid is absorbed. The rice should be light and fluffy and have steam holes on the surface. Remove the cinnamon stick and stir in the rind from 1 lime.

To make the dressing, place the bird's-eye chilli, remaining rind and lime and lemon juice, fish sauce and sugar in a food processor, mix for a few minutes until blended. Alternatively, place all these ingredients in a screw-top jar and shake until well blended. Pour half the dressing over the hot rice and toss until the rice glistens.

Slice the papaya and mango into thin slices, then place in a bowl. Add the chopped green chilli, coriander and mint. Place the chicken on a chopping board, then remove and discard any skin or sinews. Cut into fine shreds and add to the bowl with the chopped peanuts.

Add the remaining dressing to the chicken mixture and stir until all the ingredients are lightly coated. Spoon the rice onto a platter, pile the chicken mixture on top and serve with warm strips of pitta bread.

Calypso Rice with Curried Bananas Ⓥ

Serves 4

2 tbsp sunflower oil
1 medium onion, peeled and
finely chopped
1 garlic clove, peeled and crushed
1 red chilli, deseeded and
finely chopped
1 red pepper, deseeded
and chopped
225 g/8 oz basmati rice
juice of 1 lime
350 ml/12 fl oz vegetable stock
200 g can black-eye beans,
drained and rinsed
2 tbsp freshly chopped parsley
salt and freshly ground
black pepper
coriander sprigs, to garnish

For the curried bananas:

4 green bananas
2 tbsp sunflower oil
2 tsp mild curry paste
200 ml/7 fl oz coconut milk

Heat the oil in a large frying pan and gently cook the onion, for 10 minutes until soft. Add the garlic, chilli and red pepper and cook for 2–3 minutes.

Rinse the rice under cold running water, then add to the pan and stir. Pour in the lime juice and stock, bring to the boil, cover and simmer for 12–15 minutes, or until the rice is tender and the stock is absorbed. Stir in the black-eye beans and chopped parsley and season to taste with salt and pepper. Leave to stand, covered, for 5 minutes before serving, to allow the beans to warm through.

While the rice is cooking, make the curried green bananas. Remove the skins from the bananas – they may need to be cut off with a sharp knife. Slice the flesh thickly. Heat the oil in a frying pan and cook the bananas, in 2 batches, for 2–3 minutes, or until lightly browned. Pour the coconut milk into the pan and stir in the curry paste.

Add the banana slices to the coconut milk and simmer, uncovered, over a low heat for 8–10 minutes, or until the bananas are very soft and the coconut milk slightly reduced.

Spoon the rice onto warmed serving plates, garnish with coriander and serve immediately with the curried bananas.

Huevos Rancheros Ⓥ

Serves 4

2 tbsp olive oil
1 large onion, peeled and
finely chopped
1 red pepper, deseeded
and finely chopped
2 garlic cloves, peeled
and finely chopped
2–4 green chillies, deseeded and
finely chopped
1 tsp ground cumin
1 tsp chilli powder
2 tsp ground coriander
2 tbsp freshly chopped coriander
700 g/1 1/2 lb ripe plum tomatoes,
peeled, deseeded and
roughly chopped
1/4 tsp granulated sugar
8 small eggs
4–8 flour tortillas
salt and freshly ground black pepper
fresh coriander sprigs, to garnish
refried beans, to serve (optional)

Heat the oil in a large heavy-based saucepan. Add the onion and pepper and cook over a medium heat for 10 minutes.

Add the garlic, chillies, ground cumin, chilli powder and chopped coriander and cook for a further minute.

Add the tomatoes and sugar. Stir well, cover and cook gently for 20 minutes. Uncover and cook for a further 20 minutes.

Lightly poach the eggs in a large frying pan, filled with gently simmering water. Drain well and keep warm.

Place the tortillas briefly under a preheated hot grill. Turning once, then remove from the grill when crisp.

Add the freshly chopped coriander to the tomato sauce and season to taste with salt and pepper.

To serve, arrange two tortillas on each serving plate, top with two eggs and spoon the sauce over. Garnish with fresh coriander sprigs and serve immediately with warmed refried beans, if liked.

Sweet Potato Cakes with Salsa Ⓥ

Serves 4

700 g/1¹/₂ lb sweet potatoes, peeled
and cut into large chunks
salt and freshly ground black pepper
25 g/1 oz butter
1 onion, peeled and chopped
1 garlic clove, peeled and crushed
pinch freshly grated nutmeg
1 medium egg, beaten
50 g/2 oz quick-cook polenta
2 tbsp sunflower oil

For the salsa:

1 ripe mango, peeled, stoned
and diced
6 cherry tomatoes, cut in wedges
4 spring onions, trimmed and
thinly sliced
1 red chilli, deseeded and
finely chopped
finely grated rind and juice of ¹/₂ lime
2 tbsp freshly chopped mint
1 tsp clear honey
salad leaves, to serve

Steam or cook the sweet potatoes in lightly salted boiling water for 15–20 minutes, until tender. Drain well, then mash until smooth.

Melt the butter in a saucepan. Add the onion and garlic and cook gently for 10 minutes until soft. Add to the mashed sweet potato and season with the nutmeg, salt and pepper. Stir together until mixed thoroughly. Leave to cool.

Shape the mixture into four oval potato cakes, about 2.5 cm/1 inch thick. Dip first in the beaten egg, allowing the excess to fall back into the bowl, then coat in the polenta. Refrigerate for at least 30 minutes.

Meanwhile, mix together all the ingredients for the salsa. Spoon into a serving bowl, cover with clingfilm and leave at room temperature to allow the flavours to develop.

Heat the oil in a frying pan and cook the potato cakes for 4–5 minutes on each side. Serve with the salsa and salad leaves.

Vegetable Frittata Ⓥ

Serves 2

6 medium eggs
2 tbsp freshly chopped parsley
1 tbsp freshly chopped tarragon
25 g/1 oz pecorino or Parmesan
cheese (or vegetarian hard
cheese), finely grated
freshly ground black pepper
175 g/6 oz tiny new potatoes
2 small carrots, peeled and sliced
125 g/4 oz broccoli, cut into
small florets
1 courgette, about 125 g/
4 oz, sliced
2 tbsp olive oil
4 spring onions, trimmed and
thinly sliced

To serve:
mixed green salad
crusty Italian bread

Preheat grill just before cooking. Lightly beat the eggs with the parsley, tarragon and half the cheese. Season to taste with black pepper and reserve. (Salt is not needed as the pecorino is very salty.)

Bring a large saucepan of lightly salted water to the boil. Add the new potatoes and cook for 8 minutes. Add the carrots and cook for 4 minutes, then add the broccoli florets and the courgettes and cook for a further 3–4 minutes, or until all the vegetables are barely tender. Drain well.

Heat the oil in a 20.5 cm/8 inch heavy-based frying pan. Add the spring onions and cook for 3–4 minutes, or until softened. Add all the vegetables and cook for a few seconds, then pour in the beaten egg mixture.

Stir gently for about a minute, then cook for a further 1–2 minutes, or until the bottom of the frittata is set and golden brown.

Place the pan under a hot grill for 1 minute, or until almost set and just beginning to brown. Sprinkle with the remaining cheese and grill for a further 1 minute, or until it is lightly browned.

Loosen the edges and slide out of the pan. Cut into wedges and serve hot or warm with a mixed green salad and crusty Italian bread.

Index

Index